Praise for *Fiber Magick*

"A delightful guide that is full of inspiration and important information."

—Lady Willow, witch, priestess, and owner
of Willow's Pagan Shop on Etsy

"A many-layered exploration of handcrafts as magical pursuits . . . Whether you're a longtime crafter or a newbie, no matter what kind of art or craft you prefer, *Fiber Magick* will show you how to integrate your creativity into your spiritual practice for a deeper, more magickal life."

—Laura Perry, longtime weaver, spinner,
and sewist and author of *Labrys & Horns*

"From setting intentions to blessing your work, this delightful book introduces practitioners to the art of magickal *making* . . . *Fiber Magick* presents a comprehensive guide to the deep connection between handcrafts and spiritual workings, including deities associated with the domestic arts, color symbolism, knot magic, and correspondences for fabrics, textures, and the tools of the fiber crafter. The projects included are cleverly designed and richly detailed, and in ways that anyone, from the beginner to the experienced crafter, can benefit from."

—Patti Wigington, author of *Herb Magic*,
Witchcraft for Healing, and *Badass Ancestors*

"Reading *Fiber Magick* by Opal Luna was like sitting down with a cup of lovely tea, curling up in her craft room, and having a one-on-one creative class. She provides so many examples of ways to incorporate witchcraft into yarn craft, and vice versa . . . I cannot recommend this book enough."

—Stacy Psaros, Southern Strega, longtime crafter, and
technical director and columnist for *The Wild Hunt*

"*Fiber Magick* is a potpourri of magickal information! Anyone reading this will gain a true understanding of the power, reverence, and joy that can come from making one's own magickal crafts . . . The organization of the projects by skill level will help readers find the right project for them. All the correspondence charts are a veritable treasure trove of information that will aid anyone, regardless of experience, in their spellcrafting. This book will help one not only make many amazing magickal crafts, but also weave the very 'fibers' of the universe!"

—Christopher Johnson, hereditary witch elder and
co-owner of Love & Light Spiritual Emporium

"I am delighted by Opal Luna's *Fiber Magick*. The way she writes about how to bring magick into one's crafting is practical and well-suited for the various projects in the book. She covers a range of fiber and spellcasting techniques so that there will be something for both the beginner and more experienced witchcrafter as well as all those in between."

—Raechel Henderson, author of *Sew Witchy*

FIBER MAGICK

OPAL LUNA

© Sagredo Photography

About the Author

Opal Luna lives in South Florida with her husband and four cats. She is an active member of the UUCFL and Moonpath CUUPS. She enjoys crocheting and magick and teaching crocheting and magick. She blogs from time to time at Fibermagick.com and makes videos, which you can find on her Fiber Magick YouTube channel. Use #fibermagick on Instagram and join the Fiber Magick Crochet Coven on Facebook.

To Write to the Author

If you wish to contact the author or would like more information about this book, please write to the author in care of Llewellyn Worldwide Ltd. and we will forward your request. Both the author and the publisher appreciate hearing from you and learning of your enjoyment of this book and how it has helped you. Llewellyn Worldwide Ltd. cannot guarantee that every letter written to the author can be answered, but all will be forwarded. Please write to:

Opal Luna
℅ Llewellyn Worldwide
2143 Wooddale Drive
Woodbury, MN 55125-2989
Please enclose a self-addressed stamped envelope for reply,
or $1.00 to cover costs. If outside the U.S.A., enclose
an international postal reply coupon.

Many of Llewellyn's authors have websites with additional information and resources. For more information, please visit our website at http://www.llewellyn.com.

FIBER MAGICK

OPAL LUNA

A Witch's Guide to
Spellcasting with
Crochet, Knotwork
& Weaving

Llewellyn Publications | Woodbury, Minnesota

First Edition
Second Printing, 2022

Cover photo by Woodbury Picture Perfect
Cover design by Shannon McKuhen
Editing and book design by Lauryn Heineman
Pattern proofreading by Kathy Pruchnicki

Illustrations on pages 105–115 by Wen Hsu
Illustrations on pages 32, 35, and 172 by Llewellyn Art Department
Interior photos by Woodbury Picture Perfect

Llewellyn's Classic Tarot by Barbara Moore and Eugene Smith © 2014 by
Llewellyn Publications

Llewellyn Publications is a registered trademark of Llewellyn Worldwide Ltd.

Library of Congress Cataloging-in-Publication Data
Names: Luna, Opal, author.
Title: Fiber magick : a witch's guide to spellcasting with crochet,
    knotwork & weaving / Opal Luna.
Description: First edition. | Woodbury, Minnesota : Llewellyn Publications,
    2021. | Includes bibliographical references. | Summary: "71 crochet,
    knotwork, and weaving patterns for use in spellcasting and personal
    spiritual practice"— Provided by publisher.
Identifiers: LCCN 2021033544 (print) | LCCN 2021033545 (ebook) | ISBN
    9780738765426 (paperback) | ISBN 9780738765549 (ebook)
Subjects: LCSH: Witchcraft. | Magic. | Handicraft—Miscellanea. |
    Crocheting—Miscellanea. | Knots and splices—Miscellanea. |
    Weaving—Miscellanea.
Classification: LCC BF1572.H35 L86 2021 (print) | LCC BF1572.H35 (ebook)
    | DDC 133.4/3—dc23
LC record available at https://lccn.loc.gov/2021033544
LC ebook record available at https://lccn.loc.gov/2021033545

Llewellyn Worldwide Ltd. does not participate in, endorse, or have any authority or responsibility concerning private business transactions between our authors and the public.

All mail addressed to the author is forwarded, but the publisher cannot, unless specifically instructed by the author, give out an address or phone number.

Any internet references contained in this work are current at publication time, but the publisher cannot guarantee that a specific location will continue to be maintained. Please refer to the publisher's website for links to authors' websites and other sources.

Llewellyn Publications
A Division of Llewellyn Worldwide Ltd.
2143 Wooddale Drive
Woodbury, MN 55125-2989
www.llewellyn.com

Printed in the United States of America

Acknowledgments

I would like to thank all the members of Moonpath CUUPS and the South Florida Pagan community at large for encouraging me to make my passion into a practice. Thanks for playing along.

Dedication

This book is dedicated to those of us who long to put some magick back in our lives and to the folks who can see the sparkle in everyday things. Most of the projects and ideas here are inexpensive and quite achievable, even if you have yet to explore your crafty side. The aim is for you to enrich your life and embellish your world by tapping into your heart's vision. Bring it out into the material world for others to see and appreciate.

Feel the magick.

Be the magick.

Create the magick.

Contents

Project List

1. The Sacred Tablecloth
page 32

2. The Sigil Cloth
page 35

3. The Offering Bowl
page 36

4. The Ritual Cloak
page 38

5. Chakra-Balancing Bracelet
page 50

6. Chakra-Boosting Anklet
page 54

7. Elemental Prayer Beads for Grounding *page 72*

8. Triple Goddess Beads for Enlightenment *page 75*

9. Crocheted Prayer Beads
page 76

10. Picture Frame Loom
page 81

11. Nature Weaving
page 86

12. Group Weaving Project
page 88

25. Witch's Hat
page 143

26. Crocheted Poppet
page 152

27. Goddess of Journeys
page 155

28. Chakra Doll with Pockets
page 159

29. Mermaid Poppet
page 163

30. Pentagram Sigil
page 172

31. Heart Sigil
page 174

32. Goddess Sigil
page 176

33. Peace Sign Sigil
page 178

34. Angel Sigil
page 180

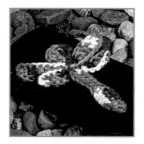

35. Dragonfly Sigil
page 182

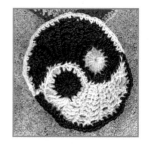

36. Yin-Yang Sigil
page 185

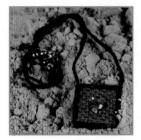

49. Amulet of Protection
page 232

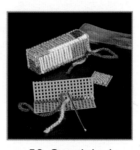

50. Door Ward
page 234

51. Besom Cover
page 237

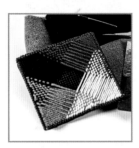

52. Ward Frame
page 238

53. "No" Sigil
page 240

54. Warrior Bear
page 242

55. Garland of Wishes
page 250

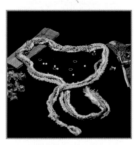

56. Handfasting Cords
page 253

57. Baby Blanket
page 257

58. Fiber Magick Star Sigil
page 260

59. Personal Pouch
page 263

60. Parent's Pouch
page 266

61. Book of Shadows Carrier
page 269

62. Remembrance Poppet
page 273

63. Samhain Spiderweb
page 278

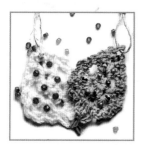

64. Yule Tree Ornament
page 281

65. Imbolc New Sprouts
Garland *page 282*

66. Ostara Egg Basket
page 284

67. Beltane Maypole Wand
page 286

68. Litha Sun Weaving
page 289

69. Lughnasadh Horned God
Poppet *page 290*

70. Mabon Mug Cozy
page 293

71. Pagan Pride Ribbon
page 296

Introduction

Magick comes from within us. It starts out as a feeling. The same can be said about art and design. Whether it comes out of desire or need, all art and innovation grow from a feeling. As this feeling matures, it takes the form of an idea. It will be so clear in the mind of the artist that it is as if it already exists. Of course, when you try to tell people your idea, many will not get it. This is your vision. You must allow it to travel from your mind's eye down through your hands to join the material world. Only then can it be shared with and appreciated by others. I call that magick. (And that's magick with a K to distinguish it from the sleight of hand kind of magic.) Calling what I do Fiber Magick makes sense. I am a crocheter, after all—a knotty, knotty hooker, if you will—and I have developed a way to turn the love of crochet into a magickal path.

My grandmother taught me to crochet when I was eight years old, so I have had many years of practicing my craft. It has grown over the years to be my passion. Crochet is a part of my daily routine. I have been certified as a Master of Crochet Stitches by the Crochet Guild of America. I teach classes in crochet and run a website, online store, and YouTube channel on the subject. I have had the pleasure of vending at conventions and festivals and seeing my workshops draw a nice crowd.

I was introduced to the Pagan community through CUUPS almost a decade ago. CUUPS stands for the Covenant of Unitarian Universalist Pagans. Moonpath CUUPS is a group that meets every Thursday night in Ft. Lauderdale to discuss a myriad of topics. I was immediately drawn to sympathetic magick, in which like brings forth like. When crocheting, I work with yarn and fabric, both natural and synthetic. I can choose from materials in a rainbow of colors in order to set my intention in my work. When you are crafting, there are numerous places where you can add intention through magickal correspondences. I could see quite clearly how my crochet could be used not only in the creation of tools but in actual spellcasting. Through the years, I have taught many classes within the CUUPS group. I have had the honor to lead rituals, sit on the leadership board of the group, and be ordained as a minister and elder in the community through Moonpath Circle.

Working with one's hands is ingrained in the human spirit, and it is what so many of us are missing. You can become hypnotized watching the string become a thing. There is a sense of accomplishment there that you cannot get from anything else. When you get in the groove, there is a calm that envelops you. A crafter will be able to understand the spirituality that I am presenting here. A piece of your heart and soul is put into an item when you truly enjoy making it, even more so when you are making it for someone else. It is quite possible that your crafting journey all started with you trying to make a gift. A handmade gift from a child is pure magick.

Once upon a time, handmade was the norm. The blanket that you swaddle your newborn babe in was probably the same one you—and quite possibly, your mother before you—found comfort in as a child. Items were passed down from generation to generation, lovingly patched or mended where needed, gathering the spirit of past loved ones. Countless lullabies and snuggles were captured. Hopes and dreams and, yes, a few worries came along with these items as they were passed down. It all added up to unconditional *love*.

Today, we live in a disposable world. Items are discarded at the first sign of character. And most often when we do receive something "handmade," it hasn't been made by a loving friend or family member, but a member of a human assembly line in a factory on the other side of the world along with thousands just like it. Where is the magick in that?

I know a man who writes computer code who says he puts his personality into his work. He understood my concept even though he was not creating anything tangible. This tells me it all starts in the head as a thought. When the thought becomes clear enough, it will move you to manifest magick even in the most mundane item.

Take a simple washcloth, for example. Now picture that washcloth filled with intention. This particular washcloth is embellished with a sigil representing the word *design*. Now when I take this washcloth into my bath ritual with me and pair it with a bergamot, orange peel, and Epsom salt mix, I am preparing myself to create new patterns.

I'm sure your mind is working now on some washcloths you would need in your life. Something with a sigil that would say "relax," perhaps, and a nice bar of lavender soap for when Mercury is in retrograde. Make a cloth with a big dollar sign on it and add a few drops of clove oil to the tub. You get the idea. Your crafting becomes the Craft. This is the basis for my Fiber Magick path. Fiber Magick is very much my witchcraft path although it has become an eclectic one due to the fact that so many different beliefs have crafting in common. If I had to choose a word to sum up my philosophy, I would choose *healer*. I imbue the items I make with energy designed to bring healing and comfort.

In this book you will learn the concept of Fiber Magick through projects using fabric, yarn, and string. Some projects will be tools to use in your magickal practice and others will be tangible expressions of the magickal working itself. Advice on how you could use each item will be given. All will be an enrichment to your path.

Many of the patterns will be presented in a magickal scenario, such as a spell or ritual. Once you have tried the project my way, there will be many opportunities to add your personality to the finished items. You will be able to refer to the lists of correspondences in the appendix at the back of this book for choices of materials and colors. Every layer of your project should reflect the intention of your desire.

Fiber Magick has proven to be quite enjoyable for children of all ages. I have facilitated many classes on the subject, ranging from the very young to the young at heart. It is interesting to see that the projects we do with the children translate quite well into projects done with an older crowd. I think that is the best thing about being part of the Pagan community. Grown people who still like to play are so refreshing in this world. Giving each other the permission to enjoy ourselves is an amazing gift. It lets our inner child grow and heal. It offers us refreshment of the soul. It makes adulting a little easier the next day.

Let's engage our inner child as well as our outer self and have some Fiber Magick fun. Let this book spark your imagination with some ways to include crafting into your magickal practice.

Hopefully, it will encourage magick practitioners to get a little bit more crafty and crafters to get a little bit more magickal.

A spiritual path for the crafter: Fiber Magick.

Part 1

FIBER MAGICK BASICS

Chapter 1

What Is Fiber Magick?

Fiber Magick is sympathetic magick elevated to an art form. There is definitely magick in handmade things. There's no way we can work with our hands and not impart some of our energy into what we make. So if this energy is going to be transferred anyway, I propose that we do so intentionally. Then by using the correspondences of color, texture, and embellishment, we can build on our intention. This is where the Fiber Magick comes in. Layers upon layers of magickal intention paint a clear picture in the mind's eye. This delights our inner child and ultimately manifests into the real world.

Fiber Magick is the practice of manifesting thought into tangible things. The layers to this practice are only limited by your own imagination. Just when you think you have dug deep enough into the fiber of your spell, you realize that you could peel off another layer. It is like a never-ending onion. The more layers you add to your intention, the clearer the picture of that intention becomes in your mind, and the more likely it will be for that intention to manifest.

Basically, Fiber Magick is an expansion of good old-fashioned knot magick. When we are crocheting, knitting, embroidering, and the like, we are tying hundreds of knots. When we are weaving, braiding, and spinning, we have the opportunity to trap energy into the fibers. The color of the cord can add meaning. Herbs and oils can be used to anoint the yarn or string. Having the moon in the proper phase, the day of the week being just right, and even being in the perfect mood will infuse those knots or fibers with intent that can be stored like charging a battery.

All this storing and charging happens automatically. Some of our energy is transferred into our work whether we consciously do so or not. So let us be aware of the energies we transfer. Art will evoke feelings in others. What do we want to convey? What is our intention in creating this piece? Whether we intend warding or healing, let's make it magickal!

Grounding and Centering

Just like in any other form of magick, preparation is the key to success. There is nothing worse than getting all excited about performing a spell or ritual and then discovering there is no sage in the house. Likewise, with crafting it is no fun to be halfway through a project and run out of the proper color thread. When doing Fiber Magick, you may need both sage and thread to be available, so make a list and check it twice. Place all your materials out on your work surface in the order of use so your working can go as smoothly as possible without breaking the momentum.

Once you have all your supplies in order, it is time to get yourself ready to do magick. How about a nice cup of tea? Set the stage for magick by consuming a little of the correct correspondence. The whole idea behind Fiber Magick is layering meaning through correspondences, so it makes sense that infusing yourself with herbs would be just as practical as infusing the yarn you are using. It might be even more effective. A nice cup of tea puts you in the proper frame of mind for magick.

You may want to take it further and enjoy a bath infused with the appropriate herbs. I suggest that you add a handful of salts to the bath as well. Salt cleanses and purifies. Epsom salt in particular adds a boost of magnesium through your skin. That is how it relieves those aches and pains. Mind, body, and spirit must be as comfortable as possible to get the best results. It would be counterproductive to try infusing a prayer shawl with healing while all you can think of is your own aching back.

Preparing to do Fiber Magick can be likened to getting ready for an athletic event. We must have our head in the game. We must be able to focus on our intention without the stress of the day getting in the way.

We do this by grounding and centering ourselves. Start by placing your feet flat on the floor. Feel Mother Earth beneath you. Now imagine roots coming from the bottom of your feet and digging deep down into the Mother. These roots go both ways, so as you breathe in, you draw up all the healing white light that you can hold. As you breathe out, you send all the stress and anxiety within you down into the ground where it can be transformed. Do this for at least three deep, cleansing breaths.

At this point, just to be sure that I have left all the worldly worries behind, I will pick up my crochet hook, make a short chain while willing my stress into the stitches, and then, taking an end in each hand, pull all my stitches out. All negativity be gone!

This is not overkill. Especially when I am making something meant for healing, I only want positive energies to get into my work. It is also a good practice to let go of all that no longer serves me each time I pick up my work. Developing this habit keeps the negativity to a minimum. This is as much for my benefit as for the finished product.

Casting a Circle

Once you are grounded and centered, it is a good idea to take a step that will keep you that way while you work. Imagine a barrier protecting you from the outside world and all its distractions. Encase yourself in a bubble of light in all directions. Left, right, front, back, up, down, north, south, east, west, above, and below—360 degrees. Enjoy this crafting cocoon for a bit, and then gather some energy to help you get to work.

Raising Energy

The world around us runs on and is made up of energy. From the photosynthesis of plants to the synapses of our human brains, sparks are flying everywhere. We can, with practice, gather this energy and focus it on our intended outcome. We can fill up our work with hopes and dreams because everything we make begins in our minds. It is time to use our imagination to the fullest.

Fiber Magick should never drain you. In fact, you should end feeling better than when you started. You first want to fill yourself with the spirit and heal yourself so that you may heal others. You want to become the conduit for the energy that comes from all around you and place it in the object. So you really want to fill yourself up with that energy first and then replenish it as fast as you dispense it. You will become the relay between all of Creation and your creation.

You may already have some experience with energy transferance. If you have ever inherited a piece of jewelry or clothing from a beloved relative, you might have "felt" them with you while wearing it. Energy will be captured in an object just from casual contact. Imagine the power that can be stored if done so deliberately.

Practice makes permanent, so practice collecting the energy around you and manipulating it. Try it with a ball of yarn. Drink in the energy through the bottom of your feet or the top of your head and direct it to where you need it to go. The technique may be different for different people because of where you see that energy coming from. It can be from a collective nature, such as Mother Nature or the Green Man. It can come from an all-encompassing godhead, such as the Goddess or the Lord and Lady. Many people call on the archangels. It's really up to you where you see it coming from, but you have to see it and you have to feel it.

Here is an example of how I do it.

RITUAL
Feel Your Inner Magick

YOU WILL NEED

A ball of yarn that fits comfortably in your cupped hands

INSTRUCTIONS

Pick up that ball of yarn and cover it with cupped hands.

Close your eyes and place your feet flat on the floor. Anchor yourself to the Mother.

Take three deep, cleansing breaths. Inhale love and light. Exhale all the stress of the day . . .

Now picture the Goddess overhead pouring crystal-clear sparkling water from a silver pitcher into the top of your head. Take note of the details. What is she wearing? How about the shape and design of the pitcher? What are her immediate surroundings? Is the water that she is pouring cool and refreshing or warm and comforting? Allow yourself to be filled up with this water of love and light. You are becoming thoroughly hydrated by this magickal elixir.

Just breathe and be filled . . .

When you are completely saturated, imagine the excess flowing from your hands and into the yarn. Begin to rotate the ball of yarn as you feel the energy transfer into it from you. The water continues to flow from the pitcher. As the energy flows from your hands, it is immediately replenished. You are the connection between heaven and earth. Continue for a while. Focus . . .

You now have a ball of yarn infused with raw energy that will need to be directed. Direct that energy by setting a clear intention for it to act on.

Setting Intention

Even though you had a reason for picking up that ball of yarn in the first place, it is crucial that you make that reason official by setting your intention to the project. This is necessary for the magick to manifest properly. You want to present a clear message to the universe for a successful outcome. Intention is always the most important ingredient in our practice. Therefore, we need to make sure our focus is true while we work.

Let us mind the words we use when stating our intentions and where we put the emphasis. When we say, "Oh, I hope it doesn't *rain*," the universe hears "rain" and says, "Yes, of course. Rain is good." But not on the day I planned my picnic! Better to sing out about how much you love a clear blue sky. Then the universe says, "Now that's a catchy tune! Let's do that."

We must also be positive in our intentions. *Want* is a negative word. It denotes that we are lacking something. If we "want" to be rich, we will be wanting to be rich for the rest of our lives. We *are* rich! And this coin purse I am making will never be empty.

Hold the ball of yarn to your forehead and see the project done. If you are knitting a scarf for a friend who is traveling to a colder climate, say out loud, "This scarf will keep them warm and free from catching cold." If you are crocheting a baby blanket, imagine the baby sleeping peacefully under it.

In the case of a larger item that will take more than one sitting to finish, it is a good idea to write that intention down. Place it with your work and refresh your intention when you pick up the project again. It is not uncommon for crafters to have more than one project going at the same time. This is a good way to keep them straight.

When creating poppets for magickal works, writing down the intention is also a good practice. The paper can then be used as part of the working. Poppets will be explored in detail later in chapter 8.

Visualization

Visualization is the art and practice of forming a mental image of something. In magick, visualization is the technique of focusing on those mental images in order to achieve a particular goal. Think of this technique as watching a movie in your head; only you control the scenes. Stopping for a moment and seeing the baby you are making the teddy bear for playing, happy, and healthy is an example of using visualization in your Fiber Magick.

We guide our thoughts to visualize the best-case scenario or use our imagination to have a full five-sensory experience of how the situation would ideally play out. Just as Olympic athletes use visualization before competitions to improve their outcomes, see a winning success even before you make that first stitch.

It helps to be in a quiet place with no outside distractions. Lie back, close your eyes, and try to picture vividly the scene you want to make happen.

Releasing Energy

Now that we have collected the needed energy, set an intention for its purpose, and visualized the desired outcome, we must release all this into our work. We do this as we make the item by directing the energy out through our hands. It may take some practice to give up all that beautiful light we have collected, but we know there is always more where that came from. Trust in the abundance of the Goddess and keep only what you need. Send the rest out to where it is needed. Send it to your project according to your intention.

Some of the projects in this book will have a string left hanging from the finished project. It is left for the recipient to cut it off or weave it in in order to accept the energy of the piece. Releasing the energy from ourselves will be vital to the success of this type of magick. We want to "move on" from these pieces to allow the magick to manifest. Doing so acknowledges that the desired results have been already achieved, no question.

Shielding

Shielding in magick is putting an invisible wall between your energy and any entity that may be harmful or draining. Visualizing an actual wall is usually sufficient. This comes in handy when you are practicing Fiber Magick where other people or distractions are around. Even if you have cast a circle of light around yourself, you may want a more substantial barrier at times.

This shield can also be visualized as a door you can close when you have gathered enough love and light necessary for the work. Use what you need and then ground.

Choosing the Proper Time

So much has been written about the phases of the moon and how they affect the outcome when casting spells or performing rituals. There is absolutely no mistaking the draw of lunar power. It affects everything on this earth, from the tides of the sea to one's menstrual cycle, some say. And if you can wait until the correct phase to perform your Fiber Magick, it would be quite beneficial.

New Moon: Time for new beginnings. Plan new projects and start them now. Think about picking up a new craft at this time.

Waxing Moon: The moon is getting bigger and so is your magick. Time to make projects for growth and abundance.

Full Moon: The powerhouse is full and ready to charge your work. If it is possible, try some crafting by the light of the full moon. Make some moon water to bless future projects.

Waning Moon: Time to banish, either by creating projects for that purpose or quite literally finishing up some of your works in progress.

But sometimes the need is immediate, and we cannot wait for the proper moon phase. That's when we can call upon the power of the sun.

The sun actually goes through phases like the moon does, but unlike the moon, the sun moves through several different phases every day. This allows the Fiber Magick practitioner unlimited opportunity for immediate spellwork. Think about the time of day you are creating your work or when you want to perform a blessing on your finished piece. The various times of day will add different energies to the project.

Sunrise: As the sun rises, this energy lends itself to new beginnings, change, and cleansing. Think of the expression "It's a brand-new day" and go with that feeling. This would be very beneficial to magickal workings that involve new endeavors, employment, love, or direction in your life. It is also the perfect time to bless a baby blanket.

Mid-Morning: As you sit on your patio enjoying your morning cup of tea, the energy of the sun expands and becomes stronger and more active. Any project that requires building, growing, or expanding works well during this phase. As the energy of the sun builds, so can the positive aspects in your life. Resolve situations in which courage is necessary, and add warmth and harmony to your home during this phase. What a nice setting in which to make your witch's ladder (see page 92).

High Noon: If you are brave enough to go outside in the noonday sun, the peak of high noon, the vibration is excellent for performing efforts that involve mental abilities, health, and physical energy. This is a time when you can charge crystals and ritual tools. Add this energy, high noon power, to the projects that you will be giving to someone who needs courage and strength.

Afternoon: In the afternoon as we perceive the sun's journey down to the horizon, its energies take on a more receptive quality. This is a good time for efforts involving professionalism, business matters, communication, and clarity.

Sunset: Now, can you imagine watching a beautiful sunset while working on projects designed to remove what no longer serves? Take this time for removal of stress, confusion, hardship, or depression. This would be the time for efforts to end a harmful relationship with a person or a substance. Move on and look forward to the new day. Every day we get a chance to say, "Tomorrow will be a good day!"

Utilizing the Elements: Earth, Air, Fire, and Water

The four elements play a big role in Fiber Magick. In chapter 7, "Basic Fiber Magick Crochet," I assign an element to each of the basic crochet stitches. Using a certain stitch will add the attributes of that element to the finished piece through association. This makes it possible to add certain attributes while being free to use any color desired. Combinations of colors and stitches will create depth of meaning. Multiple aspects of the situation can be addressed to customize spells and tools.

Embellishing

Just about every project in this book ends with you embellishing as desired. This is where you make it your own. Your embellishments will add that little spark of magick to get the job done. Appliqué becomes magick when we give intention to the image being added to the object. Creating a small bag to collect fairy gifts while on a nature walk is magickal enough. Then adding the image of an acorn adds strength and protection for your adventure. You can buy ready-made appliqués and bless them for this work or make them yourself and add many more layers to your intention.

It is a good idea to get yourself a shoebox or craft container and start an embellishment collection. You will never be able to find the exact right thing at the exact right time if you don't have this valuable resource. Keep your eyes open for doodads of all sorts. It doesn't matter that you have no idea what you will do with this bauble now. The time will come when it will be perfect serendipity.

Some things to look for are beads, ribbons, charms, buttons, and braids, of course, but remember to think outside the box: spare keys, stray washers or nuts, tassels, broken jewelry, pieces from toys, and all shiny things. Embrace your inner magpie and be ready to embellish when the instructions call for it.

Upcycling

Upcycling is a huge part of Fiber Magick. Using the old to make the new is the practice of transformation. All the energy collected over the years in old clothing, jewelry, and household items creates a foundation for whatever you add to it. When you are treasure hunting in the thrift store, "feel" as well as look for your materials. Make a trip to the secondhand store into a magickal journey by setting a goal for your quest before you get there. If you need buttons for a garment to be used in ritual, ask the powers that be to manifest what you need to find. Then keep an open mind. You may be blessed with something more perfect than you could have imagined.

Storing Magickal Supplies

The Fiber Magick practitioner, as any magick practitioner, may collect a vast array of spell components along the way. In addition to your embellishment box you will accumulate herbs and oils, yarns and cords, fabric, and so on.

I keep my Fiber Magick spell supplies separate from my regular craft supplies. Spell components are stored in a box with a piece of selenite for cleansing. My Fiber Magick emergency kit includes several balls of yarn in the colors I use most: blue for communication, green for healing or money, and pink for love. In addition, there are a crochet hook, scissors, and a cotton ball dabbed with lavender oil to produce a calming effect. This little kit stands ready to react when I hear of a need in the community.

Blessing Your Work

You can think of this step as your signature at the bottom of your masterpiece. The finishing touch ensures your hard work will accomplish its goal. The following exercise can be used for an all-purpose blessing when you have finished an item. Refer to the lists in the appendix at the back of this book for the proper color and scent choices to match your intentions.

⟞ RITUAL ⟶
Project Blessing

YOU WILL NEED
Your finished project
Incense in a scent appropriate to your intention
Candle in the appropriate color
Water in a bowl
Salt in a bowl

INSTRUCTIONS
Place the item to be blessed on a flat surface. Light the incense and place it to the east. Light the candle and place it to the south. Place the bowl of water to the west. Place the bowl of salt to the north. Hold up your work, presenting it to each direction and reciting as follows:

> *Air I am.*

Pass it through the incense smoke.

> *Fire I am.*

Pass it above the candle flame, carefully.

> *Water I am.*

Sprinkle it with a little water.

> *Earth I am.*

Sprinkle it with a pinch of salt.

> *Spirit I am.*

Hold it to your third eye.

Repeat the recitations and movements three times. Then pronounce out loud the intended purpose of the item, as in these examples:

> *This blanket will wrap them in courage and strength! So mote it be.*
> *This poppet will stand with them through hardship! Blessed be.*

Chapter 2

Inspiration, Deities, and Sacred Space

In order to do any kind of crafting, you must first find your muse. This is especially true in spiritual crafting. If you do not underestimate this powerful support, you will be amazed at the creativity that is waiting for you. The term *muse* comes from Greek mythology and has become synonymous with the word *inspiration*. It pertains to the stimulus that drives your creativity. The actual Muses were goddesses, daughters of Zeus, king of the gods, and Mnemosyne, Titan goddess of memory. Each one specialized in a category of the arts or sciences, such as poetry, music, history, or astronomy. Artists looked to them and acknowledged them as the source of their genius. Your personal muse may turn out to be a person, place, or thing. Finding this catalyst that sparks your imagination will reap many rewards.

Inspiration Around You

There are a number of ways in which you can create an atmosphere that is conducive to inspiring your creativity. You might want to go outside for a while.

It might be a spot in your garden or a bench in the park, but being anywhere out in nature refreshes the spirit. If you have the pleasure of attending Pagan festivals and conferences, you will be able to draw from that atmosphere and feeling of community. Connecting to the Mother feeds the soul. But that is not to say that the city offers no motivation. People watching in a crowded café or subway car is just what some artists need. Wherever you find your connection, enjoy it and then take it home with you in your mind's eye.

Nature can be a very powerful collaborator. Many artists use the lines of a flower or texture of a tree to enhance their designs. The spider is a good inspiration for the crafter. I see spiders everywhere and try to stop and pay homage to their magnificent webs. It reminds me of the interconnectedness of all things. The web is also a testament to the leap of faith it took to throw that first strand of silk out to catch the breeze. Throwing it out more than once if needed to finally land on a branch and stick there. Walking that tightrope to be able to form anchor lines and foundation lines and eventually dance in spirals. Lying in wait for an opportunity and snatching it. Just to gather it all up, recycle it, and start all over again. The spider is a living embodiment of the determination needed to begin again each time we get knocked down. She plays the hand she was dealt, and she does so brilliantly.

Another place where inspiration may strike is in your bed. Always keep a notepad and pencil handy on the nightstand to take advantage of any lucid dreams. A nice cup of mugwort and peppermint tea before retiring does not hurt in the least. Of course, you have to write it down immediately in order to capture the entire message. It can be added to or subtracted from later at your leisure, but you will regret it every time if you say, "I'll remember," and turn over and go back to sleep.

Listening to a piece of music can put you in the mood to create. Music can also be a brilliant ingredient to your creations. The style of a song can add the same rhythm to your finished product. Use your favorites to enhance your mood. Lyrics do not have to be included in the song to produce the desired effect. It is the feeling that we are going for here, and nothing makes you feel stronger than the correct piece of music. Usually, in a workshop I start the session with a chant. It not only sets the mood but also brings the students' attention into focus. It also connects us in purpose. There are dozens of popular chants in the Pagan community. I hand out lyric sheets, but most times they are unnecessary. We have all sung the words hundreds of times. There is power in that. Don't be afraid to rely on the familiar. It is popular for a reason. It connects like minds and souls.

Inspiration can also be found through other people's creativity. We can peruse websites that specialize in our particular craft and not even leave the house. A trip to a museum or art show can be a great springboard for your own masterpieces. The word *museum* comes from that word *muse*, after all.

Stay humble and grateful and you will attract more good things. Keep an eye out for inspiration, and it will find you wherever you are. Remember to use all three eyes. Inspiration may be waiting for you not in an actual, physical space but in a place in your heart. Take the time to lose yourself in a garden of imagination and bask in the glow of creativity. Then, just to be sure, petition some divine assistance.

Deities

There are many goddesses who will help you with your Fiber Magick. Spinning and weaving were daily chores in households before the industrial revolution. Mostly, women were called upon to perform these tasks, and it surely seemed like magick when the crafter was adept. Household goddesses blessed the hands of diligent workers. Probably because spinning and weaving were once thought of as primarily women's work, most of the patron deities are goddesses, not gods. That's not to say there were none.

As a caution, I must advise that you do your homework before calling on any deity for assistance. There needs to be an understanding of the cultural and spiritual context of a deity's worship before calling on them. Many of these deities are a part of living religions and cultures. The list I provide here should be used as a starting point for further research. If one seems to resonate with you, then do the research that needs to be done to find if working with the deity is right for you. Always be respectful of the culture of origin and make the effort to find deities related to your own. Get to know these gods and goddesses and establish a relationship with them, if appropriate. Once you have made a proper connection, be ready to channel their energy. In my experience, there will be plenty.

Because of my Italian heritage, I was drawn to explore Italian witchcraft and the Roman pantheon. I have dedicated my craft room to the Roman goddess Minerva. If that seems right for you, I highly recommend getting to know her.

Let's consider a few from all over the world and think about how they might help when it comes to crafting.

Amaterasu

Amaterasu, goddess of the sun, is one of the most important Shinto goddesses, and she rules over weaving, making heavenly clothing on her loom. She is associated with cultivation of rice and the silkworm. A sun goddess's energy would serve us well as we add the sun's energy to the work we are doing.

Arachne

This mortal was skilled, yes, but boastful and proud. Her flawless depiction of the sins and secrets of the gods got her turned into one of many spider goddesses. When you imagine yourself weaving a spell, you might hold your focused intention like the warp of the cloth and picture the steps to make it so as the weft traversing in and out as you accomplish your goal. Much like Arachne wove her tapestry, we can bring our intentions to light and life while weaving our spells.

Athena

This Greek goddess of wisdom, war, defense, weaving, pottery, and other crafts is said to have invented weaving. Her blessing would be welcome when spinning and weaving or planning a future project.

Brigid

The Celtic goddess of home and hearth inspires poetry, arts, and crafts. Her holiday is Imbolc, when she leaves signs of hope that winter will end. Fire is her element. Call upon Brigid to inspire the passion to create.

Chih-Nü

The love story of this Chinese goddess, known as the "Spinning Maiden" and "Weaver Girl," inspired the holiday called the Qixi Festival, which is like Chinese Valentine's Day. She weaves together the heavens, fate, and night and day and is said to watch over handicraft contests in the form of a spider.[1] She will grant skill to worshipers in the arts of needlework, embroidery, and making fancy flowers.

Frigg

A Norse goddess whose name means "beloved," Frigg is Odin's wife and the mother of Baldr and Höðr. She is the goddess of civilization and the true mother of all. She is also the protectress of children. She spins from the sacred distaff of life and is said to know the future, although she will not speak of it.

---

1   Justine T. Snow, "The Spider's Web. Goddesses of Light and Loom: Examining the Evidence for the Indo-European Origin of Two Ancient Chinese Deities," *Sino-Platonic Papers* 118 (June 2002): 3, 11–12, http://www.sino-platonic.org/complete/spp118 _chinese_weaving_goddess.pdf.

Grandmother Spider/Spider Woman

Many Native American cultures have myths and legends dipicting Grandmother Spider as a creatrix and friend to humans. For instance, stories are told by the Choctaw about Spider giving humans the gift of fire and teaching them the art of weaving and pottery.

Habetrot

Habetrot is a character of English folklore whose long lips were a result of her years of spinning. She is a fairy who can easily turn yarn and other fibers into clothing. A shirt made by Habetrot is considered to provide immunity to disease. She would make an excellent role model when crafting items for protection and healing.

Holda

In Germanic and Scandinavian folklore Holda is an old woman associated with spinning, childbirth, and domestic animals. The White Lady of Winter, she rewards the hard-working, as told in a Grimm fairy tale about her, "Frau Holle." Holda's connection to the spirit world through the magick of spinning and weaving has connected her with witchcraft in German folklore. She was thought to ride with witches on her distaff (a stick or spindle on which wool or flax is wound for spinning), which closely resembles the brooms that witches are thought to ride.

Ixchel

Ixchel, or Lady Rainbow, is a Mayan goddess who rules over fertility, health, and vegetation and is the inventor of painting and weaving. She taught humankind to spin and weave, and her iconography is often linked with the phases of the moon.

Kothar-wa-Khasis

An ancient Semitic god whose name means "Skillful-and-Wise," Kothar-wa-Khasis is the patron god of smithing, craft, engineering, and invention and makes weaponry for the gods.[2] He is also associated with divination and magick due to his use of incantations. His help could be useful when writing the blessings for an item.

....

2   "Kothar," Encyclopedia Britannica, last modified November 22, 2000, https://www
    .britannica.com/topic/Kothar.

Inspiration, Deities, and Sacred Space

Lugh

Sometimes called "The Shining One," Lugh is a Celtic god with mastery of all arts and crafts. Lugh is a master builder, harpist, poet, sorcerer, metalworker, and healer, and he led his people to victory in battle. He symbolizes enlightenment as he brings light to the world. Some Pagans celebrate the great god Lugh every August at Lughnasadh.

Metis

This Titan of wisdom, prudence, and deep thought is the first wife of Zeus and the mother of Athena. In one myth, Zeus fears a prophecy that claims a future son with Metis would dethrone him as he did his own father. After lying together, Zeus swallows Metis, but instead his daughter Athena is born fully formed and fully clothed from his forehead.

Minerva

The goddess Minerva was held in high esteem in the Etruscan culture. She is the Roman goddess of wisdom and the embodiment of it. She is the patroness of those who use their intellectual gifts. Minerva is not only a symbol of divine intellect; she is seen as a goddess of many skills, including crafts, poetry, commerce, and strategy. Her influence can support efforts to teach.

Moirai

The Moirai, or the Fates, are a group of three goddesses who weave the fates of mortals upon their birth: Clotho ("the Spinner"), Lachesis ("the Allotter"), and Atropos ("the Inflexible"). Hesiod describes them as the daughters of Nyx, but other sources present them as daughters of Zeus and Themis. Their power is above the influence of other gods, including Zeus.

Mokosh

Mokosh is a Slavic goddess and a protector and patron of women. She is associated with spinning, weaving, shearing of sheep, crochet, laundry, and childbirth. But she is not just a goddess of housework: she spins the destinies of women.

Neith

One of the oldest deities in Egypt, Neith created the universe. She is the goddess of wisdom, weaving, the cosmos, mothers, rivers, water, childbirth, hunting, war, and fate. Her symbol is similar to a loom, reflecting how she weaves the world anew each day on her loom.

Ptah

Ptah is the Egyptian patron god of craftsmen and architects. He is also said to be the creator of the universe. He brought things into existence through thought and speech, compared to other gods, who created things with physical methods.

Saraswati

Saraswati is the four-armed Hindu goddess of knowledge, language, music, and other arts. She is often depicted holding a book and a stringed instrument and is sometimes accompanied by a peacock, symbolizing dancing. She represents the free flow of wisdom and consciousness.

Tayet

An Egyptian goddess of textiles and weaving, Tayet is responsible for creating embalming cloth used in mummification, which also makes her a funerary goddess. She became associated with pharoahs, priests, and other officials because they wore fine linen.

Víðarr

This son of Odin is second only in strength to his half-brother Thor. He created a shoe made from the scraps of leather discarded by cobblers. Wearing this shoe, he kicks open the mouth of the wolf Fenrir. He avenges his father's death and survives Ragnarok.

Vulcan

A son of Jupiter and Juno, Vulcan is a god of fire and blacksmithing in ancient Roman mythology. During the August fesitval of Vulcanalia, the ancient Romans built bonfires and offered sacrifices to spare their crops and stores from fire. Like his Greek counterpart Hephaestus, Vulcan is a god of the forge who makes weaponry and armor for the gods.

Sacred Space

Now with our inspiration attained and the Divine called upon, we need to take a look at the environment in which we will be creating. Preparing the space can be as simple or as ceremonious as you see fit or as befits the project.

Sacred space is any space or area that has been dedicated to a sacred or holy purpose. There is no need for fancy statuary or ornate altars unless that's what will make it more sacred to you. For the most part, the Divine is imposed on the earthly through purpose. A comfortable chair with a side table to hold your tools can be all the sacred space you need to perform Fiber Magick. Just like all magick, the sanctifying of space starts with your intentions. The space in question will also be determined by how much room there is available.

If you have a designated craft room, then your search for sacred space is over. You could set up an altar so that your divine inspiration is always right there in front of you. In your craft room, all your materials would be displayed at hand's reach. Everything could be nicely spread out and convenient. A few friends could be invited over to toast the dedication.

But most of us do not have that luxury and must make do in a corner or even share the space with family. This is not a bad thing. A cozy corner makes for great ambiance while crafting. Decorate your corner with things you or family or friends have made. Encouraging family members to join you in your crafting creates precious memories. Passing your craft down the line is very rewarding.

Mobility is a nice feature when dealing with small sacred spaces. A cart on wheels that might be pulled out from a nook or closet will help keep crafting from seeming like a chore. Staying organized will encourage you to craft more. Quick cleanup will eliminate any complaints from non-crafting roommates.

Once you have determined where you will be crafting, it will be time to take an inventory of the basic needs of your craft. All crafts require a work surface and room to sit or stand while crafting. Thought must be given to storage for your materials when not crafting as well.

In the most extreme tiny-living scenarios, these needs could be covered with a folding chair and a large storage bin. The closed bin could act as a work surface. We will be making a sacred tablecloth and a sigil cloth in the next chapter. Laying one out on any flat surface will create sacred space if the cloth is dedicated to that purpose. This makes a great starting point for ritual and spellwork even before you cleanse and cast your circle.

A beneficial addition to your space is an actual altar. This altar could be dedicated to any of the previously mentioned gods or goddesses or to creativity itself. If space is an issue, it might be nice to collect six small finished craft projects that would represent the primary and secondary colors on the color wheel. If you use the crocheted sigils from chapter 9, you might include a red heart for passion, a dark orange and light orange yin-yang sysmbol because balance creates happiness, a yellow and gold peace sign because peace is smart and worth more than money, a green angel for healing, a blue dragonfly to remind you to speak your truth, and a purple third eye to wake up the magick we all have inside. All six of these sigils arranged in a circle would not take up much space and can be easily tucked away in your crafting supplies box at the end of your crafting session.

RITUAL
Dedicate Your Sacred Crafting Space

Once all the desired items have been collected and room has been reserved, it is time to make the space sacred. Your space should be clean and uncluttered. A clean area is more conducive to calm, clear thought. Dust, vacuum, polish, and declutter your workspace thoroughly. Once it is clean physically, you can cleanse it spiritually by performing this ritual.

You can buy black salt from your local metaphysical shop or online. You can also make your own by mixing regular salt with charcoal dust. And, even though a vacuum cleaner would get the job done, the act of sweeping with a broom of any kind, whether your space has carpet or not, connotes doing away with the negativity.

YOU WILL NEED
Clean work space
Black salt in a shaker
Besom or broom
Sage stick or loose-leaf sage and fireproof dish
Carnelian stone chips

INSTRUCTIONS
Stand at the edge of your space with a shaker of black salt, and ground and center. Walking in a spiral and moving into the center of your space, sprinkle the black salt on that clean floor.

Take three deep cleansing breaths as you imagine the salt sucking up any negativity.

Using your besom or broom, sweep all the black salt out of your space and out the front door if possible. If that is not practical, sweep it into a dustpan and throw it outside. (Of course, a vacuum can be used after the ritual to pick up any remaining salt.) As you do, repeat this chant:

Sweep, sweep, sweep away. Sweep, sweep, sweep away.

Light the sage and allow the smoke to get into every inch of the space.

Place the carnelian chips around your space, making sure some are in your view and others are hidden. Carnelian is the stone of creativity.

If your crafting space is permanent, leave the stone chips in place. If it is temporary or shared with others, you may want to pick up the ones in plain sight and store them with your crafting supplies.

Chapter 3

Tools of the Trade

You and your intentions are the primary tools in your toolbox. Most magick can be accomplished with your will and your hands. That being said, most magickal practices have their sacred implements that are used in rituals and spellcasting. Practitioners build their altars and fill their toolboxes with the tools of their trade, so to speak. Fiber Magick is no exception. Your collection will start with those tools necessary to do your brand of fiber art. It could be a crochet hook, knitting needles, or a tatting shuttle. Scissors, needles, and a tape measure might be included. Maybe a crewel embroidery needle will be your athame and the canvas is your altar. Though these items will take the place of athame and wand in most cases, there will be more traditional magickal tools added to the mix. Possibly, an altar cloth or an offering bowl will prove useful. No matter what, I do suggest that we should all have the chalice in common, whether it be filled with coffee, tea, or vino.

Most artists will gravitate toward a particular tool that feels good in their hands. Magick practitioners will do the same. When using your talents for straight-up magickal purposes, it is a good idea to keep a designated set of tools. These tools can be kept on your altar and be ready when needed. Repeated use will add energy to the crafting tool just as it does to a magickal tool.

The Four Main Tools of Fiber Magick Crochet

I will use the tools of crochet to demonstrate because that is what I do. Decide on the basics of your craft and substitute other crafting tools according to your needs. Any of the first three tools can be used when casting a circle around yourself before you begin working.

The Wand, a.k.a. the Crochet Hook

The wand represents the element of air or fire, depending on the tradition, and can be made from most any material. A crochet hook comes in metal, wood, or plastic. Loop after loop, you are building intention. This tool also comes in all sizes, shapes, and colors. Usually, when creating spells, the size of the finished product does not come into play. Make sure that you use a crochet hook that feels good in your hand and one that creates the smoothest experience. I suggest an H/8 5.00 mm.

The Sword, a.k.a. Scissors

The sword represents the element of air. Scissors cut out the desired portion or snip off what no longer serves. I have a tiny pair of very old scissors that reminded me of the pair that my grandmother, Lula, owned. Hers were in the shape of a stork, and I would love to come across a pair exactly like hers. Until then, I will impose the idea on the pair that I have. There is also a huge pair of metal dressmaker's shears in my tool kit for ceremonies.

The Athame, a.k.a. the Yarn Needle

The athame also represents the element of air. Use it to focus the energy into every stitch. Find a needle with a nice big eye and some heft to it. Intention will be placed with the features of a doll or connections created when sewing pieces together. I actually have two. One is sharp for piercing fabric, and the other is rounded for going between stitches.

The Chalice, a.k.a. the Coffee Cup

The chalice represents the element of water. As part of the preparation to do magick, make a ritual out of your favorite hot beverage. Refer to the list of teas and their correspondences in the appendix at the back of this book.

Additional Magickal Tools

The more tools we can actually make ourselves, the more personal and powerful our magick will be. You can add your own energy to your Fiber Magick tool kit by making the following projects.

The Sacred Tablecloth

- -

I have an old round tablecloth on which I have drawn a pentagram. I painted a pentagram in the center so that I can lay out a sacred circle no matter where I am, even if the table is square. Using the cloth over and over builds up the energy in it too.

SKILL LEVEL
Beginner

FINISHED SIZE
60"

YOU WILL NEED
60" round table cloth
2'-long string
Thumb tack
Pencil
White paint
2"-wide foam paint
   brush
Measuring tape
Yardstick or straight
   edge

INSTRUCTIONS

1 Find the center of your tablecloth by folding it in half and half again. Mark the center point and spread it out on a surface you can stick a tack into.

2 Tie one end of the string to the tack and the other to the pencil. Draw a circle out on the cloth. Go over the pencil line with the white paint using the foam brush.

3 Mark a starting point on the circle and mark off every 30 inches around the circumference of the circle using the measuring tape.

4 Use the straight edge to connect the points in the sign of the pentagram. Starting at the top, numbering the points clockwise, you would draw lines from points 1 to 3, 3 to 5, 5 to 2, 2 to 4, and then 4 back to 1.

5 Go over these lines with the white paint using the foam brush. Now you can lay it out on any surface and have a nice circle.

Make a Sacred Tablecloth of Any Size

Here's the math so you can make a symmetrical pentagram on any size circle. Circumference is pi (3.14) times the diameter. So for a circle 4 feet in diameter, the circumference is 4 feet × 3.14 = 12.56 feet. Divide this number by 5 to get about 2.5 feet. Multiply it by 12 to turn it into inches, and you get about 30 inches between the points you use to draw your pentagram. Plug in a different diameter to get the size pentagram you desire:

diameter (feet) × 3.14 = circumference (feet)

(circumference / 5) × 12 inches = distance between points on pentagram (inches)

The Sigil Cloth

‑ ‑

A sigil cloth comes in handy during rituals and spells. It is also wise to keep your tools wrapped in that sort of protection. A sigil is a symbol. It represents an idea, desire, or intention. Using the appropriately colored cloth and thread can add layers of intention. You can cross-stitch spells into your work using symbolism.

We use sigils every day. The dollar sign is quite a popular one. The peace sign is another. You can also make up your own sigils. One way is by removing the vowels and repeated letters from a word or phrase and rearranging what's left into a design. When asked about what qualities you are looking for in the partner of your dreams, you might say, "Healthy, wealthy, and wise." Here is a sigil that can be made from that concept with the letters HLTWNDS:

SKILL LEVEL
Beginner

FINISHED SIZE
12" × 24"

YOU WILL NEED
14" × 26" piece of
    embroidery fabric
Iron
Sewing needle and
    thread or sewing
    machine
Sigil
Washable marking
    pencil
Embroidery hoop
Embroidery floss
Embroidery needle

INSTRUCTIONS

1 Hem your cloth by first ironing a ½-inch double fold on all four sides of your cloth, then sewing the fold in place by hand or machine.

2 Create your sigil and draw it on the cloth with the marking pencil.

3 Embroider the sigil while focusing on your intention.

4 Forget it and know that the universe remembers.

The Offering Bowl

This little bowl can sit on your altar and collect the bits of yarn, string, and cloth from your Fiber Magick. Only place natural fibers such as cotton, bamboo, or wool in the bowl to return to the Mother.

While these instructions teach you to make a four-inch bowl, this process can be used to make bowls of any size. Just continue the flat base until the desired width is reached.

SKILL LEVEL
Beginner

FINISHED SIZE
4" diameter

YOU WILL NEED
Tapestry needle
2 yds of 4-ply yarn
2 yds of macramé cord

INSTRUCTIONS

1 Thread the needle with the yarn. Make a tiny fold at the end of the macramé cord and secure it with a few stitches.

2 Begin coiling the macramé cord, and as you do, make a stitch in to the previous round to tack it in place every ½ inch. Keep the coiled cord flat. Do not stretch it. Take a stitch through the previous round and then over the working cord. Continue to coil and tack until it is 4 inches across.

3 Continue to coil, but lay the cord on top of the previous round so that it builds sides and becomes a cup. Do this for at least 6 to 8 rounds, tacking in place every ½ inch.

4 Cut the cord, knot it in place, and cut the yarn.

Using Your Offering Bowl

If you craft on a regular basis, you will have scraps, and when those scraps are of natural fibers, they can be offered as building materials to our feathered friends. To provide a nest for the birds, you will need cloth or yarn scraps of natural fibers such as cotton, wool, and silk; wood chips (untreated, unpainted); plant materials and herb stems; and a sacred space in which to offer them. Set the bowl out in the designated area and leave it a few days so they will venture near it. As you do, recite this poem:

May I offer you these snips and scraps
To use to keep your babies warm?
We take so much from your natural home.
Please accept my offering. I mean no harm.
Build a nest from this meager stuff.
I do not want to waste a bit.
With expert skill, you can take the lot
And build a comfy bed from it.

The Ritual Cloak

You may not feel the need to don ritual garb every time you practice Fiber Magick, but for those special occasions you will want to make yourself a cloak to wear. This way when you are doing a ritual or spell that calls for it, you will be ready. This cloak will more than likely be a forever work in progress. You may want to add sigils and appliqué as your skills grow and change. Mementos of sabbats, accomplishments, or initiations will create a robe that is uniquely yours.

The idea of making a cloak may seem intimidating to the beginner, but here's an easy way to make a basic model. Using already-hemmed materials saves time and effort. A variety of patterns and colors makes it possible to match any occasion.

SKILL LEVEL
Intermediate

FINISHED SIZE
Adult large

YOU WILL NEED
2 12" × 12" cotton
   bandanas
Needle and thread or
   sewing machine
54" × 70" lightweight
   cotton tablecloth
Pins
Iron
6" strip of cloth ribbon
   or braid
2"–3" button

INSTRUCTIONS

1 Place the right sides of the bandanas together and sew across two adjacent sides to form the hood. Turn it right-side out.

2 Gather the long edge of the tablecloth with long running stitches until it measures 24 inches.

3 Fit the fabric to the bottom edge of the hood with right sides together.

4 Pin, iron in place, and sew.

5 Iron the seam flat.

6 Form a loop with the ribbon and sew it to the cloak just under the hood seam.

7 Sew the button on the opposite side of the cloak.

Dedication and Consecration of Magickal Tools

Once you have found your main four tools and anytime you have created new tools, you should dedicate them as part of your magickal tool kit. Consecrate them to a divine purpose and provide a shield of protection.

⟶ RITUAL ⟶
Dedicate and Consecrate Your Magickal Tools

Choosing the right moon phase to perform a dedication adds a layer of magick to your ritual. During the new moon is the time to start new things. It is a time of cleansing and purifying of the body and mind. On the other hand, the time during the full moon is perfect for spells related to increasing your intuitive awareness, healing magick, rituals that connect you closely with deity, or any magick related to developing your magickal skills. So, if you were to dedicate your tools at the new moon initially, then do the ritual at the full moon from time to time you would get the best of both.

YOU WILL NEED
Ritual cloak (optional; see page 38)
Sacred tablecloth (see page 32)
Tools you want to consecrate
Orange candle
Cup of peppermint tea
Sigil cloth (see page 35)
Bowl of pink salt
Nag champa incense
Pouch that your tools will fit in

INSTRUCTIONS
Wear the ritual cloak if you desire. Spread out your sacred tablecloth to create sacred space. Place your tools in the east within the circle. Place the candle in the south for the fire of creativity. The cup of peppermint tea goes in the west for pure vibrations with the sigil cloth beside it. The bowl of salt takes its place in the north for earthly healing. Set an incense burner with the nag champa in the center of the circle for balance and focus.

Imagine a ball of light hovering above the center of the table. Extend the light so that it encompasses you and the entire circle, including above and below. Stand still for a minute and allow this light to fill you.

Take a breath and focus your intention. Take as much time at each direction as you feel you need.

Light the incense. Watch the smoke rise above your altar. If you are able, breathe in the scent. Enjoy it for a while.

Light the candle. Watch the flame dance.

Pick up the cup. Breathe in the aroma. Drink deeply of the tea but leave some in the bottom of the cup.

Take a pinch of salt. Rub it between your fingers over the bowl. Watch as the crystals fall back into the bowl. Repeat several times.

Now, one by one, pick up a tool. Pass it through the smoke of the incense. Next, pass it over the flame of the candle (carefully). Then dip it in the tea. Dry it off with the sigil cloth. Finish by rubbing it with the salt over the bowl. Continue in this fashion for all the tools you want to consecrate. Remember to do the pouch that will hold these tools as well.

When you have accomplished this with all your tools, gather them up together in your hands and hold them to your heart center. As you are doing so, say these words:

We have passed through the same smoke.
We have passed over the same flame.
We have drank from the same cup.
We have touched the same earth.
We will act as one.
Blessed be!
So mote it be!

Place the tools in the pouch, but before you put them in a safe place to await your next crafting adventure, a quick spell is in order.

SPELL
Keeping Track of Your Tools

This spell will assure that your tools will be ready for you when needed. Hold the pouch to your heart center and say,

The tools of my trade become a part of me,
Extending my intention for the world to see.
Fairy friends, who hide wallets and keys,
When having your fun, please don't bother these.
And if I should lay them where they should not be,
Please help them find their way back to me.

Chapter 4

The Magick of Color

The colors and patterns bringing life to our Fiber Magick come from all around us. There is no denying that they have a strong influence on our moods and therefore our magick. The significance of choosing the right colors cannot be denied. Color is the go-to correspondence that will determine the direction of your magick. Colors can mean different things to different people, so go with your intuition. Let your use of color personalize your magick.

Basic Color Meanings

Colors have the power to make us happy or sad, hungry or angry—you name it. Once we know how they affect us, we can use them to bring about the desired results in ourselves and through our magickal practices in others. When you choose yarn and fabric, attention must be given to the correspondences relating to the various colors. The right color will improve the ability of your finished item to do the job it was meant to do.

Red Is Passion: The element of fire, sexual energy, passionate love, anger, heat, confidence and courage, strength, energy, and protection against being attacked

Pink Is Love: Romantic love, friendship, a warm family, goodness, peace, sweetness, forgiveness, and sleep

Orange Is Happiness: Joy and laughter, creativity, major changes, encouragement, confidence, warmth, enthusiasm, activity, energy, the harvest, fertility, and attracting what you need or want

Yellow Is Intelligence and Courage: The element of air, ideas, mental clarity, strengthening the intellect, knowledge, studying, business ventures, counseling, happiness, and optimism

Green Is Healing and Growth: The element of earth, wealth and money, prosperity, luck, success and achievement, healing and health, earth magick, nature and garden spells, fertility, marriage, and balancing an unstable situation

Blue Is Communication: The element of water, emotions, safe travels, loyalty, healing, relationships, peace, and tranquility.

Purple Is Magick: Intuition, spirituality, spiritual power and development, spiritual healing, invoking spirits, higher psychic ability, connecting with higher realms, wisdom, dream work, general protection, success, progress, fame, promotion, and happiness

Brown Is Grounding: The element of earth, earth elementals, communicating with nature spirits, grounding, balance, earth energies, hearth, and home

Black Is Protection and Grounding: Absorption and removal of negativity, repulsion of dark magick, banishing, uncrossing, releasing, breaking up blocks, removing hexes, letting go, and binding

White Is Purity: Cleansing, truth, protection, blessings, angels, spirituality, grace, and forgiveness. A neutral color that can be used in place of any other color.

Gray Is Neutral: Fairy magick and communicating with fairy realms, vision quests, veiling, cancellation, hesitation, balance through compromise, endurance, acceptance, knowing all things must pass, dignity, and respect

Gold Is the God: The sun, solar magick, masculinity, victory, overcoming, honor, ambition, success, power, prosperity, higher intuition, good fortune, and quick money

Silver Is the Goddess: The moon, moon magick, femininity, psychic development, divination, astral work, and insight

Now that we have established some basic color meanings, let's look at how these colors will affect the individual. Individual experiences may vary when working with colors, but in general there are colors associated with each area of the body and the organs that are in those areas. Knowing about the chakras and how their flow and balance affect people is very useful in creating magickal items.

Chakra Work and Color

Chakra literally means "wheel" in Sanskrit. Imagine a vortex of spinning energy interacting with various physiological and neurological systems in the body. Each energy center is represented by a color on the light spectrum. The attributes of those colors need to be balanced in order to have a healthy mind and body. Chakras absorb energies from the universe and nature. The chakras will also be affected by the energy from other people.

The Seven Basic Chakras

Understanding how the colors relate to the various parts of physical and emotional makeup helps us create useful tools and projects.

Root Chakra (Red): Sitting at the base of your spine, the root chakra is the seat of your basic material needs. This chakra can affect your grounding, stability, and security. Keeping it balanced could be the difference between passion and anger.

Sacral Chakra (Orange): Located at your lower abdomen, the sacral chakra is the seat of your emotions. This chakra can affect your happiness, relationships, and creativity. Keeping it balanced could be the difference between joy and despair.

Solar Plexus/Navel Chakra (Yellow): Located at your upper abdomen in the stomach area, the solar plexus chakra is the seat of your personal power. This chakra can affect your self-esteem, self-worth, and metabolism. Keeping it balanced could be the difference between pride and pridefulness.

Heart Chakra (Green): In the center of your chest, just above the heart, is the seat of all matters of the heart, love, understanding, trust, compassion, and forgiveness. Keeping it balanced could be the difference between being a friend and a frenemy.

Throat Chakra (Blue): Located in the throat is the seat of communication: listening as well as speaking. Keeping this chakra balanced could be the difference between being understood and being misconstrued.

Third Eye Chakra (Indigo/Bluish-Purple): At the forehead between your eyes is the third eye chakra, the seat of psychic abilities: telepathy, visions, and connections to your higher self. Keeping it balanced could be the difference between finding deeper meaning and remaining shallow.

Crown Chakra (Violet/Reddish Purple or White): At the very top of your head is the crown chakra, the seat of universal consciousness, the god/goddess source, and enlightenment. Keeping it balanced could mean the difference between divine inspiration and emptiness.

When you practice Fiber Magick, it is important to stay balanced. The energy you fill an item with should not be fighting against the purpose of the item. For instance, if a poppet is meant to bring the receiver courage and a sense of self-worth, the poppet maker should be aware of the condition of their own solar plexus chakra. The mental image of a sphere of yellow light will boost the project. Then afterward, do some balancing exercises to bring that area back in harmony with the rest.

MEDITATION
The Color Wheel

When balancing the chakras, it is helpful to visualize each color blending into the next. This harmonious flow of energy will break up the blockages that might keep a chakra closed. Focusing on each color in turn reduces the risk of becoming unbalanced to the point where we exhibit the negative characteristics of any chakra. A good way to do this is with meditation.

The following guided meditation encourages the flow from one color to the next. Use it to balance yourself in preparation for crafting. It is a good idea to record this meditation so you can close your eyes and picture the scene in your mind. After the meditation, there is a bracelet project designed to help keep that balance in check.

Begin by taking three deep breaths. Now, plant your feet on the ground and feel your roots sinking deep into Mother Earth. When you are rooted in the Mother, your mind is free to travel. You can journey using your mind's eye. Explore your flights of fancy. Remember, you can always safely return to this place.

Imagine the most beautiful garden setting. Not too sunny. Not too dark. Not too warm. Not too cold. In every way, this garden is perfect, a perfect balance of nature. Imagine yourself standing in the center of this garden.

All of a sudden, you notice one red flower. As you contemplate this red flower, you feel that color deep down within you. This red becomes your passion, and you feel a zest for life and an excitement for what is coming next. As you look around, you see more and more red flowers. It becomes a little overwhelming, and you begin to feel agitated. Maybe a little angry. Your passion needs to be tempered.

As you keep looking, you notice that there are also orange flowers. As you contemplate these orange flowers, you begin to see creative ways to vent that anger, creative ways to use that passion. You become happy at the thought. As your mind plays through all these happy and creative ways that you are going to use your passion, you begin to get a little silly. Then you become a lot sillier, and your creativity gets off the chain, creating all these wild thoughts, ideas, plans, and dreams. It becomes a little too much because you know that half of this stuff is never going to happen. And that is when you begin to notice the yellow flowers.

The yellow flowers add intellect to your creativity, and though you did not notice them before, the red flowers are still there, as are the orange flowers. The yellow flowers join them, and together your intelligent and passionate creativity begins to blossom. This is what was needed, this yellow flower. You begin to notice that there are more and more yellow flowers everywhere. You start to feel the need to study more, to know more, to know everything, until you realize that you are trapped inside your own head. Suddenly, you are collecting so much information that you will never be able to use it all.

But just before you become discouraged, you notice that every one of these flowers has a green leaf. You begin to heal yourself. Your passion, creativity, and intellect all blend into a beautiful bouquet. The green healing leaves surround and intermingle among them. You feel great. You feel whole. You feel healed. If there was only a way everyone could feel like this, a way you could share this healing. That is when you notice the blue butterflies.

Fiber Magick is similar to candle magick. Colors, herbs, and oils all add meaning. We usually light a candle before beginning our work. Fire safety cannot be overemphasized. Never leave a burning candle unattended. For long burns, place a candle in a safe place, like the kitchen sink. Never place a candle cozy on a bare pillar candle, only one with a glass cylinder. Stay crafty and safe.

The blue butterflies land on each flower and each leaf, whether red, orange, yellow, or green. You have added communication to your healing, and now you can share it with others. You attend healing circles and study groups. You share everything that you have learned, and there is a give-and-take. There is sharing and there is caring. You are manifesting this good work in your community. And as you do, you notice some of these butterflies are purple.

That is the magick. You have come full circle back to your passion. And you notice one . . . red . . . flower . . .

It is time now to leave this beautiful garden, though you can return again at any time you like. Feel the roots you have sent to the Mother draw back up. Take another three deep, cleansing breaths and return to reality.

Chakra-Balancing Bracelet

Now that you have come full circle through the meditation, create a token that will keep you balanced even on a trying day.

In this project, we will be tying the knots from left to right and adding a bead between each knot. As we do so, we will be feeling the energy of each chakra as it travels up our spine in conjunction with our working on the cord. In this way the beads and knots act as a reminder of how it feels to balance each chakra center. This will take as long as it takes, so do not rush. You are putting in the work now so that later when it is needed, you can call that balanced chakra to mind quickly.

SKILL LEVEL
Beginner

FINISHED SIZE
12"

YOU WILL NEED
24" of cotton cord or
    yarn
7 colored beads that
    correspond to each
    of the chakras
Safety pin (optional)

PREPARATION
Make sure the length of cord will wrap around your wrist at least three times. Keep in mind that the thickness of the cord and the size of the hole in the bead will have to be taken into consideration. You may find that you must double the knot in order to keep the beads from slipping past it. If so, work that into your spell by making one knot before the meditation and one after. You may want to do that anyway. Maybe even three times for emphasis.

I like to use gray cotton yarn for this project. Cotton connotes protection and healing. Gray is a neutral color that artists use to bring out the true color of other colors.

Lay out the seven beads in the corresponding chakra colors and a safety pin to use as a closure. You could also tie the cord around your wrist, but you would have to cut a longer piece and leave longer, knot-free ends.

INSTRUCTIONS

1 Leaving 6 inches at the left end, tie your first knot. As you tie that knot, say these words:

> Cotton cord both strong and true,
> Hold together these traits anew.
> First knot tying up the end,
> Catch my intentions from the wind.

Slip the red bead up against the knot and imagine a red pentagram or spiral at your root chakra. Make that image spin clockwise faster and faster, until it bursts into a shower of red sparks.

Take a deep, cleansing breath and say these words:

> Red as fire, passions spark.
> Light my way through the dark.
> Add this flame of love to me.
> Tie a knot in it. So mote it be.

Continue in this fashion: Tie a knot and imagine the transition into the next color. Add a bead and imagine the swirls and sparks of this new color. Take a breath and recite the words.

2 Make the second knot for the sacral chakra and add the orange bead.

> Orange, happy, joie de vivre,
> Creative juices flowing free.
> Add this surge of ecstasy.
> Tie a knot in it. So mote it be.

3 Make the third knot for the solar plexus chakra and add the yellow bead.

> Yellow, clever as a fox,
> Draw true wisdom from bones and rocks.
> Intellect coming back times three.
> Tie a knot in it. So mote it be.

4 Make the fourth knot for the heart chakra and add the green bead.

> Green brings healing to mind and soul.
> Peace and comfort be the goal.
> Bring out all the best in me.
> Tie a knot in it. So mote it be.

5 Make the fifth knot for the throat chakra and add the blue bead.

> *Blue as the ocean and sky above.*
> *As above, so below in perfect love.*
> *Oh, that I may act goddessly.*
> *Tie a knot in it. So mote it be.*

6 Make the sixth knot for the third eye chakra and add the indigo/bluish-purple bead.

> *Indigo magick and mystery,*
> *Third eye open wondrously.*
> *Reveal this power unto me.*
> *Tie a knot in it. So mote it be.*

7 Make the seventh knot for the crown chakra and add the violet/reddish-purple or white bead.

> *Violet calls the stars and moon.*
> *Heaven with the earth attune.*
> *Make me one with deity.*
> *Tie a knot in it. So mote it be.*

8 Make the eighth knot to secure the lot.

> *Wrapped around my wrist and arm,*
> *Keep me healthy, free from harm.*
> *Happy, clever, magick me.*
> *Tie a knot in it. So mote it be.*

9 From your root to your crown, all seven colors are swirling and dancing, leaving the perfect colored light where needed. As they spiral faster, they meld into pure white energy, nourishing your soul and refreshing your spirit. Your bracelet is complete.

You need not wear it as a bracelet. You can also pin this little charm to the inside of your bag or jacket. When the day threatens to unbalance you, take a deep breath. Take it in your hand and remember your happy place.

Chakra-Boosting Anklet

There may be times when you need to give one chakra or another a little boost. When you see signs of an underactive area in your flow, an effective way to refresh is to wear the needed color. You can go all out with a monochrome outfit or be a little more subtle and choose the appropriate color chakra anklet for the situation. An anklet can be worn quite inconspicuously under long pants. No one needs to know it's there but you. The following crocheted chakra-boosting anklet could be the answer. See page 105 for the crochet stitch and abbreviation guide.

I made an ankle bracelet in blue for those days when I need to be quick with my answers and explain myself clearly. This is primarily important when I'm doing a class or workshop, but speaking your truth is a good goal every day.

Make an anklet in each color to be ready for anything life throws at you.

SKILL LEVEL
Beginner

FINISHED SIZE
12"

YOU WILL NEED
2 yds of blue cotton yarn
9 blue beads
Crochet hook size H/8 5.00 mm

PREPARATION
Refer to the crochet stitch guide starting on page 105. Take a look at "Fiber Magick by the Numbers" starting on page 117.

INSTRUCTIONS
1 String the beads onto the yarn.

2 Leave a 9-inch-long end for tying.

3 Make a slipknot.

4 Ch 9.

5 Bring up a bead and make a Ch over it. Repeat 9 times.

6 Ch 9.

7 Fasten off, leaving a 9-inch-long end for tying.

8 Tie around your ankle while imagining the swirls and sparks and reciting the words for the throat chakra from the chakra balancing bracelet spell. Cut off any excess yarn and place it in your offering bowl.

Advanced Color Work: Dyeing

More magickal intent can be added to magickal workings by dyeing the fibers you are using with natural vegetable materials. This way, the properties of the plant used in the dyeing process are absorbed into the very fibers of your finished item. These energies give a boost to the magick. For instance, onion skin makes the most beautiful golden brown when dyeing cotton crochet yarn. And the onions will add the correspondences of prosperity, stability, endurance, and protection where needed. If you use this yarn to crochet the little angel sigil on page 180 of this book, it will become a guardian angel.

The amount of time and effort that goes into dyeing the fibers adds to the energy of the finished product. This is where the saying "It's the thought that counts" comes alive. It is like saying to a person, "I think you're worth my time and a messy kitchen." If time is not a factor, one technique to dye cotton yarn is to crochet or knit it up into a square or rectangle. As you do, you can set intention and store energy as usual. Then dye it as you would any cloth. Soak it in the cauldron for a solid color yarn or dab on multiple colors with a big paint brush for variegated yarn. Sigils and runes can be hidden underneath the finished color. When the cloth is dry, unravel it. Do so as a further step in the process and not as an act of banishing, which we will discuss later in chapter 7.

Wind it in a ball and use it to make a magickal item already infused with not only your energy but also the attributes of the dye. Of course a hank of yarn can be dyed and dried in less time with less effort. In either case, use caution and be aware that the natural dyeing materials may be a concern due to allergies. Make sure you are not using something to which the recipient could be allergic.

The spellwork begins with the idea's conception. Make gathering plant material for dyeing an adventure and, therefore, part of the magick. Refer to the lists of plant materials for dyeing in the appendix at the back of this book to decide what you're looking for. Once all things are considered and choices are made, it is time to begin the process. Whether your collecting is done in the forest or the grocery store, treat this as your quest.

At the farmer's market, look on the discount rack. A bruised onion still carries protection as well as a beautiful color. It also feels good to think you may be giving purpose to something that might have ended up being thrown away. Save the pretty veggies for the dinner table.

In no way natural but just for fun, Kool-Aid can be used as a dyeing agent. Along with the bright colors, you also add a pleasant scent to your project.

You will want to soak the fabric or yarn in a color fixative before the dyeing process. This will help the color set into the fibers. Natural dyeing takes some doing. It is not a quick process. Muslin, silk, cotton, and wool work best for natural dyes, and the lighter the color of the fabric the better. White or pastel colors work the best. When dyeing yarn, make sure it is secured in a hank. You can do this by wrapping it around the back of a chair and tying it in several places so it stays loosely wound. Care should be taken not to let it get tangled. Let it dry completely and slip it back over the chair before untying. Then you can more easily unwind it from the hank into a ball.

The pot that is used for the fixative will not be harmed, but it is best to use an old pot as your dyeing vessel. It will become stained and not good for much else, but it will have character. You may even choose to consecrate it as part of your magickal tools. Every witch needs a cauldron, after all.

Natural Dyeing

Taking the time to perform all the proper steps will pay off in the end. Preparation and perseverance are key. Get ready to stir that cauldron for a while, dearie. Just a note: wear rubber gloves to handle the fabric that has been dyed, as the dye can stain your hands. And unless you are tired of the existing hues of your unmentionables, all dyed fabric should be laundered in cold water and washed separately from the rest of your laundry, at least for the first wash or two.

For the fixative, use a salt fixative for berry dyes in a ratio of ½ cup of salt to 8 cups of cold water. Use a plant fixative for plant dyes, with a ratio of 2 cups of vinegar to 8 cups of cold water.

To make the dye, you will need enough water to cover the fabric or yarn being dyed. The ratio of water to plant material is two to one. So if you need one gallon of water to cover, you will need enough plant material to loosely fill a half-gallon container. The dye bath can be diluted with more water if it boils down too much.

YOU WILL NEED
Fabric or yarn to be dyed
2 large pots, at least 4 quarts
Fixative
Water
Plant material for dyeing
Rubber gloves
Strainer or slotted spoon
Tongs (optional)

The Magick of Color

Instructions

1 Add fabric to the first pot, containing the appropriate fixative, bring it to a gentle boil, and simmer for 1 hour. Drain, ring out the fabric, and rinse it well in cool water.

2 Meanwhile, chop the plant material into small pieces. Place it in the second pot. Cover with water, bring to a full boil, and then simmer for about 1 hour.

3 Remove the plant material with a strainer or spoon.

4 Add the fabric or yarn to the second pot.

5 Simmer until the desired color is obtained.

6 Gently stir occasionally to assist with an even dye. Be careful when dyeing yarn so as not to tangle it.

The color of the fiber will be lighter when it is dry. For a stronger shade, allow the material to soak in the dye bath overnight. Rinse thoroughly. Hang to air dry.

Tie-Dye: Waste Not, Want Not

Leftover dye bath can be saved in a squeeze bottle and labeled according to color and plant material used. Use these dyes to do tie-dyeing. Prepare the fabric or yarn with the fixative as instructed for natural dyeing. Twist or knot the fabric and secure it with rubber bands. Gently lay the yarn or fabric out, still tied in a hank. Use the squeeze bottles to apply the dye in a random pattern. Leave space between the colors for the dye liquid to spread. Add more in small doses so that colors will overlap and create new colors without becoming too mottled.

I like to do this in a shallow container, like the ones that fit under a bed. When I'm satisfied with the colors, I close the lid and let it sit overnight. The next day I rinse the material carefully and hang to dry. The tie-dye patterns I create will have a bearing on what type of magick the finished item will perform.

Patterns

Patterns are very closely related to color. Some patterns will read as a certain color even though they contains more colors than one. In those cases they will take on the attribute of the main color with undertones of the supporting colors' attributes. Patterns can evoke emotions, symbolize ideas, or draw attention. Some have long, brilliant histories, such as tartan plaids, which signify a family or region. Others, like our tie-dye beauties, are full of fun and frolic. The floral pattern of that old couch in the basement can bring you back to your childhood, and mandalas are a treat for the eyes as well as the soul.

Mandalas

A mandala is a spiritual or ritual geometric configuration of symbols serving as a map to deity. Examples of this art form exist in Hinduism, Buddhism, and Shintoism. The intricate designs serve as a labyrinth through which you work your way to the palace of the Divine.

A form of mandala called the yantra is similar and uses fewer colors, but it also connects the user with deity and is a meditative aid.

These designs can be painted on paper, wood, stone, cloth, or even a wall. In some traditions, such as Tibetan Buddhism, very precise and elaborate designs are created from colored sand. The Maya created round calendars with geometric patterns around a central face.

The word *mandala* is Sanskrit for "circle." This makes a lot of sense. Even though it may be dominated by squares or triangles, there is a concentric structure. Mandalas are circular designs symbolizing the notion that life is neverending. They contain a balancing visual of elements symbolizing unity and harmony. Mandalas are used for meditation purposes, allowing the individual meditating to become one with the universe. The visual appeal should absorb the mind in such a way that chattering thoughts cease. This leaves room for the more philosophical or spiritual thoughts. In short, a mandala can be hypnotic, letting the creative hemisphere of our mind run a little freer while our analytical mind takes a little nap.

The Crocheted Mandala

I truly enjoy crocheting mandalas. I love to randomly choose colors and see how it all ends up. Oftentimes I'm not comfortable with the design while it's happening, but then after it's finished, I look back and I think, *Wow, that really came together beautifully.* I let the universe use me to create. This is a good exercise for me because it is not unusual for me to dislike something that I am working on. I will be halfway through a project, and I just cannot see the end. It makes me very anxious about how it will turn out. Once upon a time I might have given up, but over time I have found the determination to carry on and am more often than not glad that I did.

When crocheting a mandala, you start at the center. The center should be a color that represents the Divine to you. You can then work your way out using the chakras or rainbows as your guide, or let the universal act of random-ness decide for you. Now is the time to use up those leftover balls from previous projects. Change colors as often as you like. Every row or every other row could be a different color. There are also yarns on the market that are dyed in long color runs that will decide when to change for you. I have included a crocheted mandala pattern on page 134.

For those who don't crochet—yet—drawing a mandala can be quite liber-ating. There are many adult coloring books on the market now that use mandala designs to get you started. The use of colors as you fill in the spaces can be either random or intentional. It's all up to you, but I encourage those who are more rigid in their designing to try their hand at letting go and building the colors randomly. You just might be pleasantly surprised with the end result.

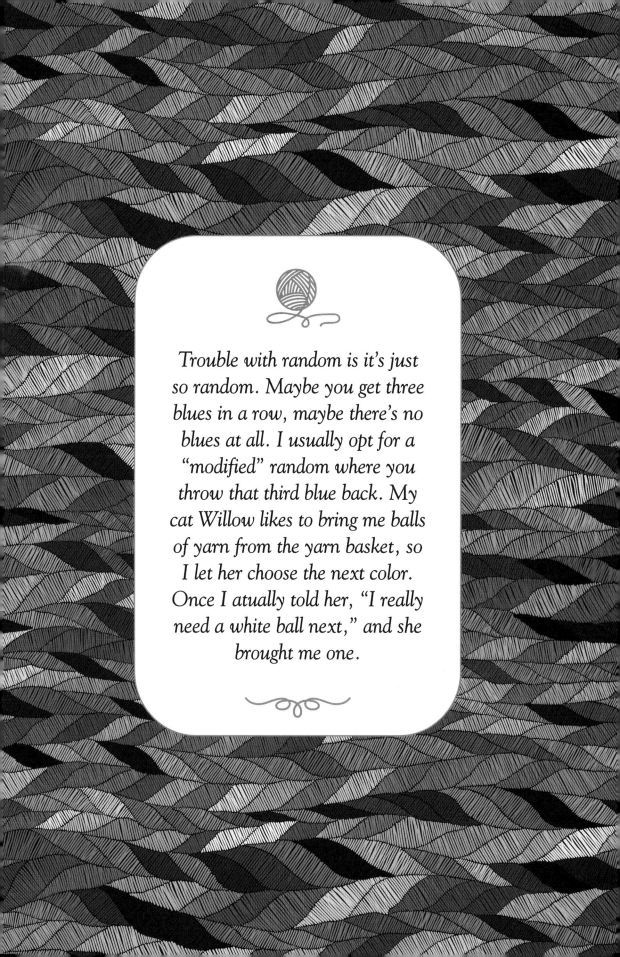

Trouble with random is it's just so random. Maybe you get three blues in a row, maybe there's no blues at all. I usually opt for a "modified" random where you throw that third blue back. My cat Willow likes to bring me balls of yarn from the yarn basket, so I let her choose the next color. Once I atually told her, "I really need a white ball next," and she brought me one.

Part 2

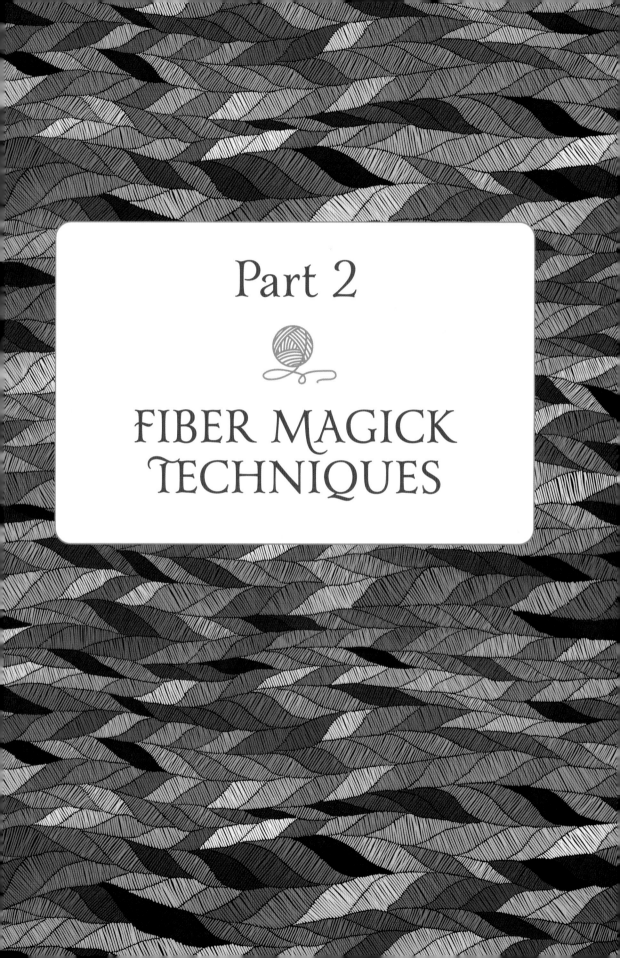

FIBER MAGICK TECHNIQUES

Chapter 5

Knot Magick

Knot magick is the ultimate magick of convenience. Energies can be stored away for future use. Spells can be cast well in advance at the most appropriate time and then used when needed.

The following spell is an example of simple knot magick. Practice this basic sequence of knots to perfect your knot placement. I have determined the length of the cord as twenty-seven inches to give you three inches to work with for each knot. You may find that you need more at first. With practice, you will be able to put those knots right where you want them.

SPELL
Basic Knot Magick

I recommend you use a cord in your favorite color for practice. This way you will be less likely to become frustrated if the knots are not cooperating. Paracords make a good practice tool because you can easily loosen the knots and replace them.

You Will Need
27" of cord
Safety pin

Instructions

1 Knots are tied in this order: 1–6–4–7–3–8–5–9–2.

Tie your first knot at the left end of your cord. Place a safety pin in this knot to mark it as the first one you tied.

2 Tie your second knot on the right end of your cord.

3 Tie your third knot in the middle of your cord.

4 The fourth knot is tied between the first knot and the third knot.

5 The fifth one is tied between the third knot and the second knot.

6 Knots 6, 7, 8, and 9 go between every other knot from left to right.

Knot Rhyme

The following is quite a popular rhyme to recite while tying the knots. I've seen many variations in books and on the web. The actual words you use do not matter so much. What matters is the progression and the building of power with every knot you tie.

> By knot of one, the spell's begun.
> By knot of two, it cometh true.
> By knot of three, so mote it be.
> By knot of four, this power I store.
> By knot of five, the spell's alive.
> By knot of six, this spell I fix.
> By knot of seven, events I'll leaven.
> By knot of eight, it will be fate.
> By knot of nine, what's done is mine.

When untying the knots to release the stored energy, untie them in the same order you tied them. This way, the energy builds up to the ninth and most powerful knot. The reason why the ninth knot is the most powerful is that you will have your intention well-focused by the time you tie that final knot.

Embellishing Knot Magick

The color and the fiber content of the cord you use can add layers to your magick. In this way, correspondences are made, creating a clear picture of intention. Oils or herbs can be rubbed onto the cord. Apply them from each end of the cord toward the middle to increase the positive energy. Consult the lists of correspondences in the appendix at the back of this book to decide on the substances that will customize your cords and enhance your magick.

Keeping a coil of cord ready for emergency situations would be quite proactive. Place a skein in a box with a sprig of rosemary for healing and protection and a cinnamon stick to repel any negative energy, and be ready the next time you hear of a friend or loved one in need.

Let's bring the age-old practice of knot magick into the modern day to see how we can benefit from tying our intentions into knots. This string of knots tied with intention can act as a talisman of protection and bolster our courage. Here is an example of a magick spell using knots.

SPELL
Up, Up, and Away! Knot Magick

This talisman will bolster courage and produce a calming effect when flying in an airplane. Create this talisman on a Thursday. No matter what day you plan to take your trip, Thursday is the best day for travel.

YOU WILL NEED
Cedar incense
27" of yellow cord
1 drop of clove oil
Safety pin

PREPARATION
Become familiar with the basic knot magick spell.

Center and ground yourself. Breathe deeply. Relax and think positive thoughts about traveling. Have some soft meditative music playing in the background. Light the incense.

INSTRUCTIONS

1 Breathe deeply. Close your eyes and imagine yourself feeling safe and secure.

2 Anoint your cord with a drop of clove oil for protection.

3 Tie the first knot according to the basic knot magick spell (see page 66).

4 Place a safety pin on this knot so you will know where you started later.

5 Continue to tie the knots in order while visualizing a safe trip. By the time you have tied that ninth knot, you are already at your destination in your mind's eye, safe and sound.

6 Chant the following words:

> *Like the birds on the wing*
> *And the clouds in the sky,*
> *I soar through the air.*
> *I will fly, I will fly!*
> *Safely, we land back on the ground,*
> *Back to the earth, safe and sound.*
> *So mote it be!*

You can carry this cord with you in your pocket or tie it around your wrist, and it may be enough to keep you calm during your flight. If at any time a little turbulence causes you to become concerned, do not panic! Just take out your cord, take a deep breath, and imagine yourself safely at your destination. Recall the feelings that you had when you tied that first knot, and slowly, with intent, untie it. Allow the energy that was stored there to wash over you and calm you down. This may be all it takes, but you have eight more to go, if necessary. If you have tied those knots tight enough, it might take you the rest of the trip to untie them. Any leftover knots can be put back in your pocket and used on the return trip home.

Simple knot magick can be performed with any type of cord and anointed with the oil that will get the job done. Any number of knots can be tied in accordance with your will. See the lists of correspondences in the appendix at the back of this book to choose the colors, numbers, and materials that will add intention to your spell. There is also a list of the best type of spell to do on each day of the week.

Binding with Knot Magick

There may be times when you do not want the knots to come undone. This may be in the case of binding or projecting a permanent outcome to a situation. In binding magick you are either binding (attaching) yourself or someone else to someone or something or binding (stopping) the actions of someone or something. You can also bind (stop) a person from coming near you. There may be good reason that you need this person to stay away. Regardless, you are affecting free will and great thought should be put into your decision to do so. I find it more acceptable to add a twist of positive when binding by keeping the desired results of the binding in mind while I work the spell.

For instance, making a knotted cord with the intention of empowering Mother Nature against the harmful acts of humans would make a great Earth Day project. Imagine these practices being stopped in their tracks as you tie each knot. While binding a negative like fracking, you could imagine the beautiful hillside that this will make possible. By the ninth knot, the harmful act is no more, and the clear picture of result is all that is left. These knots should never come undone.

Some ways in which to ensure the knots stay tied would be to burn the cord, bury it in the earth, or throw it into running water. Please be mindful of the environment as you do. Use natural fiber if burning, burying, or throwing so that harmful chemicals are not released into Mother Earth. Also, make sure the cord is not going to be a hazard to wildlife.

⸺ SPELL ⟹
No Harm to the Mother Binding

Fracking, deforestation, pipelines, plastics, run-off, emissions, littering, wasting water, and depleting the ozone are just a few dangers to the environment. Consider each one, bind it in a knot, and think about how wonderful the outcome would be.

YOU WILL NEED
27" of natural fiber cord
Sprig of fennel
Cauldron or other fireproof vessel
Lighter

INSTRUCTIONS

1 Anoint the cord by rubbing the sprig of fennel from each end to the center. Fennel guards against evil and provides strength, protection, and purification.

2 Tie each knot in the order of the basic knot magick spell (page 66), visualizing the binding of the harmful act of human greed with each knot. Between each knot, take a deep breath and imagine the beneficial results.

3 As you tie the ninth knot, declare,

> *I bind these acts in word and deed*
> *That harm the Mother through human greed.*
> *I see a future bright and clear.*
> *Harm to none is practiced here.*

4 Burn the cord in your cauldron.

Knot Magick Time Bomb

Another use of knot magick is something akin to a time bomb. Place an intention, lying in wait, for the person who unties the knot. Once upon a time the ribbons around a scroll or the ties on a parcel would be classic places to do this sort of knot magick. Woe to the individual who dares to steal from the witch who has placed a ward on their belongings in such a way. Today we have the custom of ribbons on a gift box or the straps around a journal for which we could use this technique.

Of course, it is our intention that is the most important ingredient in our magick, right? So, in addition to protecting your property, this practice could be used to bestow a wish or blessing on the recipient. Think about this the next time you tie a bow on a package to give as a gift. Would it not be nice to untie the bow and be showered with well wishes? Wishes of good health on a get-well gift, wishes of prosperity to the newlyweds, or wishes of years of happiness at the housewarming? I like that idea. Don't you?

Beads and Knot Magick

Beads come in a vast array of colors and textures. They can be made of plastic, paper, wood, crystal, or stone. Adding beads to your work is yet another way to practice sympathetic magick through correspondences. And beads have been used by many cultures in spiritual practice for millennia. The act of knotting beads onto cord is magickal in itself, and then the resulting set of beads can be used in your magickal practice.

Prayer Beads

Prayer beads provide a physical method of keeping count of the number of times a chant, prayer, or mantra is repeated as the chanter moves their fingers from bead to bead while the prayers are recited. Not having to keep track of the count mentally allows the mind to be free to meditate on the mysteries. The concept crosses a number of belief systems, from the Catholic rosaries to the Buddhist malas. The number of beads varies by religion. Some sets of Islamic prayer beads have 100, three groups of 33 plus 1, to represent the names of Allah. A Catholic rosary consists of 59 beads to keep track of repeated prayers. I used the model of the Buddhist malas to design three different sets.

Buddhist malas contain 108 beads. One larger bead is at the end to signal turning so that the prayers can be done with eyes closed. Then, back you go chanting another 108 times. That seems like a lot, but really, I did the math and 108 is a multiple of 3. That could be useful in spell work. Other ways to look at 108 would be 9 times 12, or 27 sets of 4. These combinations lend themselves to a wide variety of meditations.

The act of stringing that number of beads and arranging them to your purpose infuses energy into the finished item. A variation can be made for different purposes. The next two projects use color as part of the process, so these beads would not necessarily be used with your eyes closed. As you create them, stay focused on the purpose that the strand will perform.

Either of these prayer bead sets can be made from inexpensive materials, such as cotton yarn and pony beads, or something a bit fancier, such as satin ribbon and semiprecious stones or crystals. The color intention will still be there just the same, but the stones and crystals would add their own correspondences as well. In either case you can tie the ends together to form a circle if you like. Where it is tied will alert you that you have done a full round, and a fancier version could be worn as a necklace.

Elemental Prayer Beads for Grounding

First up, let's make a set for grounding. The next time you need some serious grounding, grab these beads and chant "Earth, air, fire, and water" twenty-seven times.

SKILL LEVEL
Beginner

FINISHED SIZE
24"

YOU WILL NEED
36" of cord that the
  beads will fit on
  snugly
Yarn needle
108 beads, 27 of each
  color: red, yellow,
  green, and blue

PREPARATION

Place your feet flat on the floor and send roots down into the Mother. Take a deep breath and draw up healing energy from your roots.

INSTRUCTIONS

1 Starting 9 inches away from the left end of the cord, tie a double knot.

2 Place the needle on the cord and string a set of 4 beads on the cord in the color pattern green, yellow, red, blue. As you do, chant,

   Earth, air, fire, and water.

3 Pass the needle through the last bead in the set again in order to secure it.

4 Bring up another set of four beads and secure the last bead.

5 Continue in this way until all beads are placed in sets of four.

6 Make a double knot to secure the beads.

7 Cut the cord, leaving 9 inches.

8 Pull your roots back up from the earth and send all the energy that you do not need yourself into the beads.

Triple Goddess Beads for Enlightenment

This is a prayer bead set for chanting "Maiden, Mother, Crone" thirty-six times as a prayer for enlightenment.

SKILL LEVEL
Beginner

FINISHED SIZE
24"

YOU WILL NEED
36" of cord that the
  beads will fit on
  snugly
Yarn needle
108 beads, 36 of each
  color, white, red, and
  black

PREPARATION
Imagine a white light of energy beaming down from the heavens and into the top of your head. Breathe deeply as you allow the light to fill you.

INSTRUCTIONS

1 Starting 9 inches away from the left end of the cord, tie a double knot.

2 Place the needle on the cord and string a set of three beads on the cord in the color pattern white, red, black.

3 As you do, chant,

> Maiden, Mother, Crone.

4 Pass the needle through the last bead in the set again in order to secure it.

5 Bring up another set of three beads and secure the last bead.

6 Continue in this way until all beads are placed in sets of three.

7 Make a double knot to secure the beads.

8 Cut the cord, leaving 9 inches.

9 Shield the top of your head and send all the energy that you do not need yourself into the beads.

Crocheted Prayer Beads

I crocheted a version using lace agate beads (8 mm) and blue cotton crochet thread. Stringing the beads and pulling three beads up at a time, I crocheted each set together with a chain stitch. I spaced the clusters with three more chains. I single crocheted back, one single crochet stitch in every chain and one in each cluster. Then I connected the ends with a larger bead made of tiger's eye (10 mm). I wore it as a necklace to a full moon drum circle to consecrate it.

Basically, the correspondences working for me as I use or wear those prayer beads are cotton (healing), blue (communication), brown (grounding), lace agate (self-acceptance), and tiger's eye (courage). And the number three is for the Triple Goddess.

See page 105 for the crochet stitch and abbreviation guide.

SKILL LEVEL
Intermediate

FINISHED SIZE
32"

YOU WILL NEED
1 large bead
Beading needle
1 oz (125 yds) of cotton
    crochet thread
Crochet hook size D/3
    3.25 mm
108 beads

INSTRUCTIONS

1 Starting with larger bead, string all beads on the thread with the beading needle.

2 When you are 9 inches from the end, make a slip knot and Ch 3.

3 Pull up 3 beads and Ch to form cluster.

4 Ch 3.

5 Repeat clusters and chains for remaining small beads.

6 Ch 1 and turn.

7 Sc in each chain and cluster across.

8 Pull up the larger bead and Sl St into the opposite end, making sure you have not twisted your work.

9 Do another round of Sc in the same thread or a different color.

10 Fasten off and weave in the ends.

I'm sure you will think of some color and bead combinations that are meaningful for you. The number of beads can be customized as well. In the appendix there is a list of deities and the numbers associated with them. If you wanted to make beads representing Yemaya, for instance, you could do sets of seven beads in colors of the ocean.

Chapter 6

Weaving and Braiding

Every time two strands of fiber cross paths, there is an opportunity for magick. Weaving and braiding have gone hand in hand with magick for millennia. Spinning wheels and looms are the stuff of fairy tales as well as creation myths. Even the simplest braid holds the power of three. I'm reminded of the common phrases used to describe magickal acts and the fiber arts, such as "weave a spell" and "spin a yarn."

Weaving

When I lay out my raw materials, crystals, herbs, and oils, I imagine them coming together just like the threads in a piece of woven fabric.

As I put them together, I might chant,

Under, over, around and through,
Back and forth, we weave anew.
Hither and yon, to and fro,
Weave a spell and make it so.

When you imagine yourself weaving a spell, you might hold your focused intention like the warp of the cloth and picture the steps to accomplishing your goal as the weft traversing in and out. Much like Arachne wove her tapestries, we can bring our intentions to light and life while weaving our spells. Further, the act of actual weaving can be a magickal experience.

I enjoy all types of meditation. One in particular involves using a small swatch of loosely woven fabric. Find a piece small enough to hold in your hand comfortably, one with a loose-enough weave that you can see the threads and how they interact. Ask yourself these questions: Is it a simple weave with the weft dancing over and under in a very uniform pattern? Or is it more complicated than that, with a strand being skipped here or there? If the fabric is more than one color, how does the weave create the pattern? Or is the pattern printed on top without a care for the weave? How does all of this reflect the interconnected web of which we are all a part? Are you the warp or the weft?

You can make yourself a simple loom on which you can create your own fabric to practice this sort of meditation. Play with textures to create abstracts to contemplate. The loom will look quite nice hanging on the wall between meditations as well.

Picture Frame Loom

Look for a frame that has some depth to it. This will give you more room to weave your needle over and under the warp yarn. The nails should be long enough to give yourself some wiggle room, and a nail with a flat head will keep the yarn from slipping off.

SKILL LEVEL
Beginner

FINISHED SIZE
10" × 12"

YOU WILL NEED
Ruler
10" × 12" wooden
  picture frame
42 1¼" flat head nails
Hammer
Marker

INSTRUCTIONS

1 Find the center of the short side of frame and place one nail there.

2 Measure and mark off nail placement at ½-inch intervals on either side of this nail. You should be able to fit ten nails on either side of the center nail on a typical 10 × 12-inch frame.

3 Repeat steps 1 and 2 for the other short side of frame. Take care that each nail is directly across from the corresponding nail on the opposite side.

4 Hammer the nails across the top and bottom of the frame at the marks.

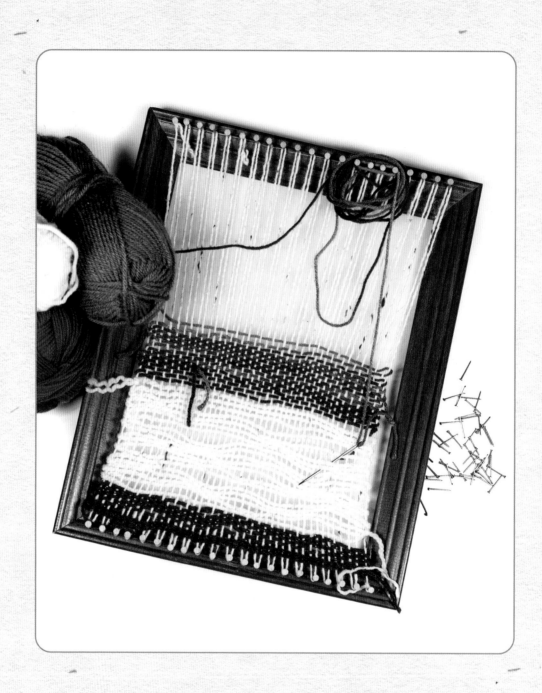

Using Your Picture Frame Loom

In weaving, warp is the lengthwise thread in a cloth, while weft is the transverse thread. The warp strands are held in tension on a frame or loom. The weft strands are drawn through, inserted over and under across the lengthwise warp strands.

You Will Need
15 yds of yarn in desired color
15 yds of various-textured novelty yarns
Large tapestry needle
Scissors
2 12" dowel rods (optional)
Craft glue (optional)

Instructions

1 String the warp by tying the plain yarn to the first nail in the top left corner of your frame.

2 Bring the yarn down and wrap it around the corresponding nail on the bottom side. Bring the yarn back up to the next nail on the top and then down to wrap around the next nail at the bottom, and so on. Continue in this way until all nails are strung.

3 Tie the yarn to the last nail.

4 Weave novelty yarns of different textures across these strands to create the weft. Be careful not to pull the weft too tight. You want your work to maintain the width of the loom. Experiment with the patterns you can make by changing the colors or textures of yarn as you go.

5 There is no need to tie the crosswise strands. When you come to the end of a strand or want to change colors, just cut and add a new piece. You can leave the ends hanging or tuck them in.

6 Your piece can be hung as is on the frame, or if you want to remove the piece from the loom, take each loop off its nail and slip them all on a 12-inch dowel rod. Do the same at the bottom. Place a drop of craft glue on the back of the four outside loops to secure. Tie a piece of yarn to both ends at the top for hanging. Use the bottom dowel to hang a fringe or beads if desired.

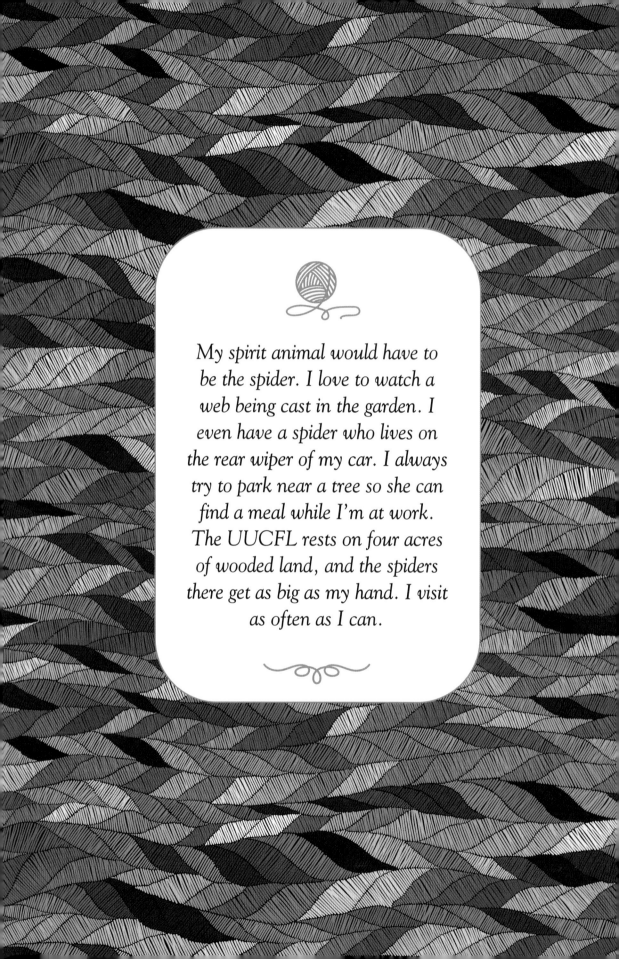

My spirit animal would have to
be the spider. I love to watch a
web being cast in the garden. I
even have a spider who lives on
the rear wiper of my car. I always
try to park near a tree so she can
find a meal while I'm at work.
The UUCFL rests on four acres
of wooded land, and the spiders
there get as big as my hand. I visit
as often as I can.

Creating Plaid

Weaving plaid is fascinating in that you end up with more colors than you started with. As the colors combine and intertwine, they will read as secondary colors.

You Will Need

Frame loom
15 yds each of 3 different colors of yarn
Large tapestry needle
Scissors

Instructions

1 String the warp, alternating two of the colors every five nails.

2 Weave the weft by alternating all three colors every five strands.

How many different squares did that create? How did the interplay of colors make new shades? Try assigning attributes to the colors and see if they change accordingly.

Nature Weaving

- -

This project is magickal even before the weaving begins. First, you will have to go out into nature and find the materials needed. Make it a time of meditation and recharging. Look for deadfall and ask permission of the spirits there before you take anything out of the woods. Use only natural materials in your piece if possible. The finishing embellishments can be any leaves, small stones, or flowers you find along the way. Reeds and grasses make wonderful weaving materials.

It would also be nice if you returned the finished piece to nature, where it could be used as a nest or shelter from the sun, wind, or rain, so use only natural fibers.

SKILL LEVEL
Beginner

FINISHED SIZE
Varies

YOU WILL NEED
Forked branch
15 yds of sturdy string
    to act as the warp
Variety of natural fiber
    yarns for the weft
Nature embellishments

INSTRUCTIONS

1 Tie the string to one of the tines where they separate.

2 Wind the string around one tine, then the other, until you reach the top of the tines.

3 Weave the yarns over and under the wound strings.

4 Weave your embellishments in between the criss-crossed threads.

Group Weaving Project

A small group can work some Fiber Magick to-gether by using weaving in its various definitions. This would be agreat activity to include in a ritual for the goddess Minerva, Brigid, or Arachne. In fact, this could be for a combination of the three. We will be using the strategic planning of Minerva when we set out the project and perform it with precision. Using the clouties of Brigid, we will form the web of Arachne.

The finished project can be used as a focal point during spells and meditations, so a collec-tion of materials from your group is desirable. Ask the participants to bring their own strips of fabric, charms or beads, but have plenty on hand for all. The space in the center would be a nice place to put a pentagram or a picture of a person, place, or thing that could stand to be surrounded by your community. Use this piece to showcase your pur-pose when doing spells or rituals as a group.

PREPARATION

When your group gets together to create the weav-ing, take a little time for socializing, keeping the con-versation on the project at hand, a bonding activity for the group. At this time you may want one person to read an appropriate meditation or piece of poetry so that everyone is in the same mindset.

INSTRUCTIONS

1 Place the smaller ring within the larger ring flat on the table.

2 Participants will gather around the table holding hands. Ground and center with three deep breaths.

3 Participants will choose a length of yarn or ribbon that they want to add to the warp of the project and tie one end to the small ring. Everyone will be doing this together, so cooperation is involved. While this is going on, the designated person will say,

> *Individually capable and strong, doing what's right, staying on their path, adding their warp to the fabric, adding their spirit to the whole.*

4 Each person will tie the other end of their ribbon to the large ring, pulling the warp taut but working together to make sure that the small ring stays in the middle of the large ring. Everyone's warp should be the same length. While this is going on, the designated person will say,

> *Together capable and strong, doing what's right, staying on our path, securing the warp while keeping all centered, becoming the spirit of the whole.*

5 Time to add your strips. Weaving the web clockwise, each person picks up a strip and begins to weave, passing their strip to the person on their left and taking up the strip of the person on their right until all strips have been woven and the space between the two rings is full. While this is going on, the designated person will say,

> *Ready to relinquish control to another while taking up the slack for the good of the whole.*

6 Time to embellish. Everyone can go crazy with their bits of yarn, string, ribbon, charms, and whatever else they have brought to add to the mix.

7 Stand back and admire your masterpiece. Comment on what you have created as a team.

Braiding

Braiding makes for a powerful spell because it requires concentration and offers lots of opportunity to pour your intentions into a physical object. By the power of three, braiding focuses on the repetitive movements to bind together what you have assigned each strand to represent, such as you, a new job, and money.

To mindfully perform this linear style of weaving, it is helpful to secure the three strands together first by tying the ends in a knot. Then anchor the knot to a flat surface using tape or a safety pin. This will allow you to focus all your attention on the braiding itself.

Using your dominant hand, pick up the outer strand on that side and pass it over the next to become the middle strand. Then, using your other hand, pick up the outer strand on that side and pass it over the next, making that one the middle strand. One more time with your dominant hand and you will have put all three strands in play. This will be repeated to braid as many sets of passes that you need to express the intention desired. (See page 118 for a list of correspondences implied by each number.)

Witch's Ladder

A witch's ladder is a string or cord that has been knotted or braided while casting a spell. Usually, feathers are stuck through the knots. Talismans of this type could be hung as a protection or a curse depending on the intent of the witch.

The following ladder is an exercise in visualization. We will be visualizing a happy home and thinking about all the puzzle pieces that go into building one. The preparation for this ladder takes longer than the actual execution of the project. But the more thought you put into it, the better the outcome will be, so take your time.

SKILL LEVEL
Beginner

FINISHED SIZE
24"

YOU WILL NEED
3 3' strands of yarn
  or twine in different
  colors (red, white,
  black)
9 pony beads or beads
  that slide easily
  on your cord in
  colors (according to
  intention)
Small twigs or sticks
Feathers

PREPARATION

Start by cutting 3 strands of yarn or twine, each 3 feet long: a strand of red for passion, one white for purity, and one black for protection. You will also need 9 beads in different colors to represent all the positive elements you want in your home. Beads with a large hole are most desirable.

Red Not just in the romantic sense, although I want that for sure, red holds passion for life so I do not end up falling asleep in front of the TV every night.

Orange My home will be a place filled with joy and laughter. Guests will feel comfortable and glad to be invited.

Yellow Uplifting conversation and the sharing of knowledge will be the norm in my home.

Green Thanksgiving to Gaia. Let me remember my place in the balance of nature. There will be abundance and health in my home.

Blue I imagine calm waters, peaceful and tranquil. May I never thirst. I speak my truth and seek first to understand in my home.

Purple Fill my home with magick and all the possibilities it brings.

Black I can be mindful of any obstacles that might exist, but I imagine them flattened. I keep a level head and do not overreact in my home.

White White welcomes guidance from the powers that be. The Goddess dwells within my walls.

Gold/Silver This represents whichever deity speaks to me. (If you would like, introduce yourself to a deity who is considered the protector of the home, such as Hestia or Brigid, and ask that they oversee your efforts to make your home everything you desire.)

The materials you choose for the rungs adds yet another layer to the magick, and these cement those puzzle pieces together.

Although feathers are very traditional in witch's ladders, be careful when gathering feathers in the wild and only do so if the law permits it. The Migratory Bird Treaty of 1918 prohibits the harming of birds in any way to collect feathers. Keep in mind that the birds use those feathers to build their nests too. Remember: harm none. Your best bet will be with the feathers of that illustrious bird the *Crafticus storicus*. That bird comes in all colors, shapes, and sizes, and gleaning its feathers does not hurt anything. Feathers will add the element of air as well as the properties of the color.

Twigs are also a good choice for rungs. Look for deadfall under the trees and take note of the tree it comes from. You can also use some herbs for this purpose. I like to save the twigs from my basil when harvesting the leaves for recipes. Basil adds healing and prosperity to the home. Pine needles do the same while also including fertility and grounding. Use cinnamon sticks for energy, creativity, and spiritual growth. Add some rosemary sprigs for cleansing, healing, and mental focus. An additional benefit is that your ladder will smell good. Sometimes, just to add a bit of fun, I might use a popsicle or lollipop stick.

Now, imagine your home. Take a few minutes to really visualize it and what it is like to live there. Is it everything you would like it to be? Using the elements we just discussed, fill in the blanks until you have a mental image of a safe, loving, nurturing sanctuary. Keep this image in your mind's eye as we bind those properties into the braid and use the beads like puzzle pieces to create the bigger picture.

INSTRUCTIONS

1 Tie your three strands together at one end with an overhand knot, secure to a flat surface, and begin braiding the three aspects together: passion, purity, and protection. Balance the three in your mind as you braid the strands together, left strand over center, then right over center, just like braiding hair.

2 After you have completed four sets of three passes for an emphasis on stability, add a bead to the center strand, then continue braiding.

3 Continue in this pattern of braiding four sets of three and then adding a bead.

4 When all the beads are braided in, tie another knot at the other end to secure it.

5 Rungs for your ladder are next in order. You can slip thin twigs and feathers through each bead. Larger items like popsicle sticks can be slipped through the braiding on top of the bead.

6 Hang your ladder by slipping the top knot over a hook or nail. Make sure you will be able to see it from time to time and remember what your home should be.

Ladders can be made for other purposes as well. Use silk and satin ribbons in colors such as green and gold to attract money and rolled-up dollar bills as the cross rungs. You may want to make more than one of these witch's ladders.

Floral Crown

The witch's ladder is a project that combines braiding (the yarn and beads part) with weaving (the rungs). This next project incorporates both as well.

These crowns are perfect for any of the sabbats. Make one for Imbolc, Ostara, or Litha by using the appropriate flowers and grasses. They can also translate nicely at Lammas and Mabon with corn husks and wheat shafts. Samhain calls for darker things like black roses or possibly a little mandrake root. Yule must have holly or mistletoe.

The floral section of the craft store will have all the seasonal elements that you need for your crown, or you may want to gather materials on your next nature walk.

SKILL LEVEL
Beginner

FINISHED SIZE
Adjustable

YOU WILL NEED
Wire snips
6' of 10–12 gauge
    metallic wire
Floral tape
Ribbons
Flowers on stems,
    grasses, and plant
    materials for weaving
2' of 20 gauge wire
Beads and
    embellishments
Floral craft elements

INSTRUCTIONS

1 Cut 3 lengths of wire 2 feet in length.

2 Twist the 3 together for 4 inches at one end.

3 Wrap the end with floral tape to secure as well as cover the pointy parts. Stretch the tape a bit as you go, and it will stick to itself.

4 Turn the twisted end under to form a 1-inch loop.

5 Braid the wire into a wide, open, loose braid.

6 Twist the ends, cover them with the floral tape, and turn the twist under to form a 1-inch loop just like you did at the other end.

7 Cut lengths of ribbon and tie them to the loops on each end. You will use these ribbons to tie the ends together, leaving the long tendrils to hang at the back of your head.

8 Weave the plant material of your choice through the wire braid. Use the 20 gauge wire to secure the stems, grasses, beads, and other embellishments.

Cloth Yarn and Rag Rugs

Rag rugs are made by braiding together lengths of cloth yarn. We can add our choice of intention to existing fabric when making the cloth yarn.

The energies in fabric will come from the fibers it is made from as well as the color it was dyed and what was used to get that color. We can also find energy when we upcycle fabrics from existing articles of clothing or household items. You can utilize clothing and household items that have been loved and enjoyed (in other words, well used). You can make them into something filled with all those feels. If you are using items found in a thrift store, you may want to pass some sage smoke over them just in case. Of course, my rule of thumb is no matter how pretty it is, if it gives you a yucky vibe, leave it alone.

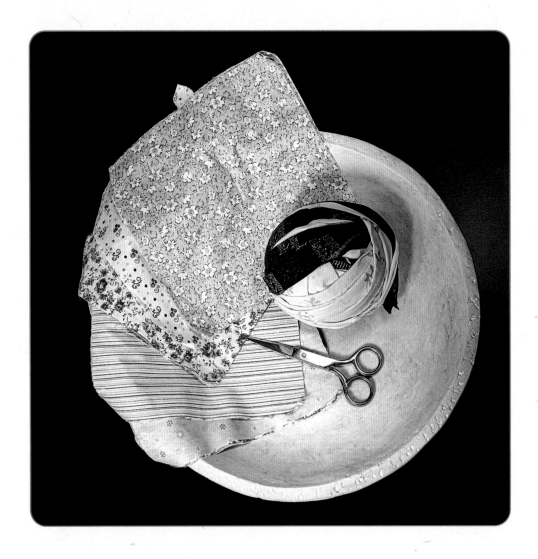

Cloth Yarn

The type of fabric we use to start with can set the stage for the magick. Picking just the right materials is the foundation that intention rests on. Assigning a type of cloth to an element speaks volumes before we even pick up a needle or scissors. The most readily available, and in many ways the most desirable, material is cotton. Cloth made of cotton adds protection to the finished item. Cotton can be safely burned or buried with no detrimental impact on the Mother.

Think about the astrological sign of the person for whom you are crafting. Can you picture a texture that matches their personality? You may want a loose weave for the laid-back individual, but you could also use that weave for the not-so-laid-back person to encourage them to relax a bit. There are lists in the appendix at the back of this book to help you make decisions.

SKILL LEVEL
Beginner

FINISHED SIZE
Varies

YOU WILL NEED
Piece of fabric that doesn't fray too much
Fabric paints or markers
Good pair of cloth-cutting scissors
Iron
Sewing needle
Thread

INSTRUCTIONS

1 Infuse your intention into the fabric by drawing symbols on it with the fabric markers.

2 Cut the fabric into 2"-wide strips.

3 Fold and iron each side in ½".

4 Overlap the ends of two strips and sew a few stitches to secure.

5 Repeat until all the strips are sewn together.

6 Divide the yarn into three balls so you can braid them together in order to make the rag rug on the next page. It takes about 10 yards of fabric to make a 24 × 36" rug. There are about 4 yards of usable fabric in a full-size bedsheet, so you don't have to really spend a lot if you are recycling.

Braided Rag Rug

- -

Set an intention while using the cloth yarn made in project 15 and create a braided rag rug that can be used for yoga or meditation.

SKILL LEVEL
Beginner

FINISHED SIZE
32"

YOU WILL NEED
3 balls of cloth yarn
Safety pins
Sewing needle
Thread

PREPARATION
Make cloth yarn from 10 yards of the fabric of your choice (as detailed on page 99).

INSTRUCTIONS

1 Grab an end from each of the three balls, overlap them, and sew them together. Take a safety pin and pin this edge to a couch cushion or other sturdy fabric item that you can use to secure the braid as you work. Keep the wound balls fairly close together (keeping them in a box on the floor works), and braid the strips together, moving backward a bit as you work.

2 Coil the end of the braid so it looks like a snail shell, pin that together, and sew it to keep it all in place. Just keep coiling and pinning, and then use a needle and thread to sew all the coils together. Tuck the last bit under the rug and stitch it in place.

Chapter 7

Basic Fiber Magick Crochet

From the very first time you pick up hook and yarn, it is possible to do magick. Even if you have never crocheted before and don't plan to make it your passion as I have, I suggest you please give it a try. There is a certain amount of magick in the act of crocheting itself. Think about it. You wave a stick, mumble a few words, and voilà! A potholder appears. I often bring my crocheting to CUUPS (Covenant of Unitarian Universalist Pagans) meetings, and out of the corner of my eye, I catch people watching my hands more intently than I am. It is fascinating to watch someone do work with their hands. Working with your hands is ingrained in the human spirit, and it is what so many of us are missing. You can become hypnotized watching the string become a thing. There is a sense of accomplishment there that you cannot get from anything else. When you get in the groove, there is a calm that envelops you. You may just find your bliss.

Whenever I tell people that crocheting relieves stress, they scoff. Okay, learning to crochet may be a bit stressful. Like everything else, it is what you make of it. Your attitude will make a world of difference in your success. Go into this as you should everything: with confidence. I have shown dozens of folks the basic movements involved in this type of craft. All too often, I see stiff, jerky attempts at controlling the yarn. Those poor knots are pulled so tight, there will be no hope of a second row. They will make that yarn mind even if it kills them. Usually, all it kills is their enthusiasm to learn to crochet. Breathe! Relax your shoulders and this will actually be good for you. Success and stress relief only come, however, after they have relaxed and allowed the hook to glide past the loops and gather the makings of the next stitch in line—sacred movement that culminates in a tangible expression of intent.

Of course, I do admit that attention must be paid to the counting of stitches, especially when turning your work around to go back the other way. One tip I always suggest is to make the counting part of the exercise. Count like you are trancing along, leaving the outside world behind. If someone tries for your attention, just count louder.

Reading Patterns

For the first half of my crochet life, I never used a pattern. I made hundreds of granny squares. I looked at the pictures and did my best to make something like it. I made up my own teddy bears and blankets without writing anything down. Sometimes I was able to reproduce the item. Sometimes I was not. Crocheting by "ear," so to speak, just like I sing.

A new world opened up to me after I forced myself to understand the crochet pattern. It was much like learning a new language, and I now speak fluently. So can you. There are many, many videos on learning to crochet and how to read patterns. I watch videos like this all the time to keep learning and incorporating new ideas and techniques into my work. I'll leave you to that but with this one thought: crochet patterns have been using textspeak for generations. All you have to do is break the code, and it will get a lot easier.

A second part of that code will be to understand the designer's phrases. There is no universal style when it comes to writing crochet patterns. What makes sense to one may not be readily understood by another, so I will translate a common phrase that you will see in my patterns: "{2 Hdc, Hdc 4 times} around." This means you put two half double crochet stitches in the first stitch and one half double crochet stitch in the next four stitches, and repeat that pattern for the entire round. If we are working in rounds, each line will begin "Rd."

If we are working back and forth in rows, each line will begin "Row." Crochet instructions would be very long if we did not use abbreviations.

I have developed a Fiber Magick crochet stitch guide that teaches the basics of crochet, as it introduces ways to use each skill in your magick. This way even mastering the foundation chain will feel like an accomplishment and add a layer of Fiber Magick to your path.

Stitch Guide

The following is a list of each stitch or action starting with the abbreviation you will see in the pattern (if applicable), then the longhand explanation, and the magickal correspondence.

Yo—Yarn Over

Grab the yarn with the hook in order to add any additional loop or in preparation of pulling it through the work. The expression used for the later action is to "pull up a loop."

Every time you yarn over and draw more yarn into your work, you can imagine gathering the energy from the universe. Tuck it inside your work all nice and cozy.

Ch—Chain Stitch

Yarn over and pull the yarn through the stitch on the hook.

The chain stitch is your foundation, so it translates well into grounding. This is where you can set your intention for the project and state its purpose. It is also the beginning of any project, so it signifies potential.

Ch Sp—Chain Space

A chain space is the space made by chaining and skipping stitches on the previous row or round. Any number of chains can be made, and the same is true about the number of stitches skipped. You may have a chain 1 space (Ch 1 Sp) or chain 2 space (Ch 2 Sp), for example. When a pattern calls for stitches to be made in a chain space, the hook is inserted in the space itself and not the chain or chains.

Sl St—Slip Stitch

Insert the hook into the stitch or space indicated, yarn over, and pull the yarn straight through the loop on the hook.

The slip stitch is basically a chain stitch you lay on previous stitches. It adds another layer of stability. I have associated it with the element of earth.

Sc—Single Crochet

Insert the hook into the stitch or space indicated, yarn over, pull up a loop (you'll have two loops on the hook), yarn over, and pull the yarn through both loops on the hook.

Rising just one chain higher than the foundation, the single crochet stitch represents the water that lies on the earth. This stitch is easy to manipulate and takes shape well, just like water.

Hdc—Half Double Crochet

Yarn over, insert the hook into the stitch or space indicated, yarn over, pull up a loop (you'll have three loops on the hook), yarn over, and pull the yarn through all three loops on the hook.

Half again higher than the water, the half double crochet dances like fire. Yarn over, pull through, yarn over, and pull through all three loops. Imagine the flames forming patterns in your work.

Dc—Double Crochet

Yarn over, insert the hook into the stitch or space indicated, yarn over, pull up a loop (you'll have three loops on the hook, as shown in A), *yarn over, pull the yarn through two loops on hook,* and repeat between * * once more (B).

The double crochet stitch is higher still. Let it be the air. See how it creates a fabric that can be woven through. It breathes.

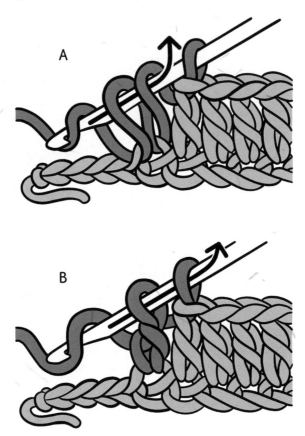

A

B

Trc—Triple Crochet

Yarn over twice, insert the hook into the stitch or space indicated, yarn over, pull up a loop (you'll have four loops on the hook, as shown in A), *yarn over, pull yarn through two loops on hook,* repeat between * * twice (B).

The triple crochet stitch must be for the Triple Goddess, of course. Chant "Maiden, Mother, Crone" as you yarn over and pull through again and again and again.

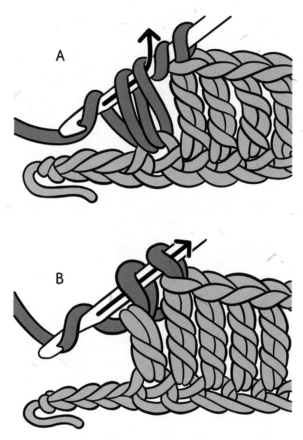

BLO and FLO—Back Loop Only and Front Loop Only

When you look down at the top edge of the row or round you are working into, you will see a series of Vs. Normally, the hook is inserted through both of these loops. Working the next row in either the back or front loops only leaves a ridge on the opposite side that can be used for shaping or decorative stitching.

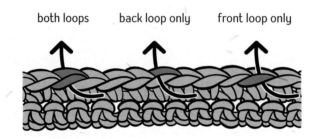

Rev Sc—Reverse Single Crochet

Working from left to right, insert your hook into the previous stitch and single crochet backward. The reverse crochet, or crab stitch, as some folks call it, is my favorite way to finish off my work. It is like when you back stitch on the sewing machine. My ninth-grade home economics teacher used to say, "Do you want it to stay sewn? Then you must back stitch!"

So if you want your spells to stay "sewn," you must crab stitch! When the spell should stay contained in your work, use reverse single crochet.

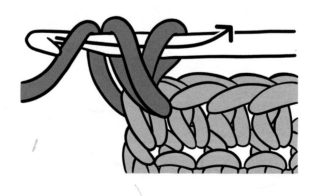

Shell

A shell is when more than one stitch is placed in the same stitch on the previous row or round. The number of stitches determines the intention. There is a list of numbers and their correspondences in the appendix at the back of this book.

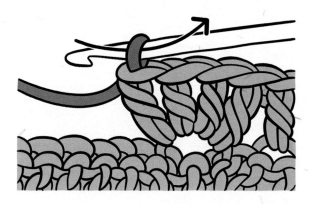

Picot

Chain 3 and slip stitch in same stitch.

Whenever you want to put a finer point on something, use a picot.

Surface Stitches

There are two ways this can be done. Sigils and accents can be added in either way.

1 Hold the yarn source underneath the work and draw loops up through the crocheted fabric, creating a chain on the top of the fabric.

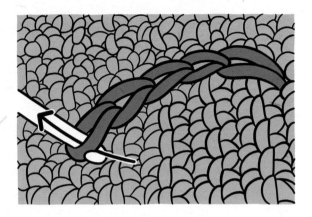

2 Hold the yarn source above the crocheted fabric and work stitches (Sc, Hdc, Dc, etc.) into the front of the fabric.

V St—V Stitch

A V stitch is made by placing 2 Dc in the same space with 1 or more chains between them. The number of chains determines the intention.

Rd—Round

Rounds can be spirals that continue to grow by the number of stitches needed to create your intention. Rounds can also be finite, and the number of rounds will be what's significant.

Tog—Together

You will sometimes need to decrease the number of stitches in a row or round when shaping. And the two shall become one. Or three or four or five shall become one.

( )—Group

Parentheses in patterns in this book usually have the same function as in regular writing, but they can also be used to indicate grouping stitches together that are meant to go into one stitch or space and to indicate how many stitches are in a row or round.

{ }—Repeat

Repeat everything between these two brackets. Any repeated pattern is a great opportunity for chanting.

Making a Slipknot

All crochet projects, regardless of skill level, begin with a slipknot. This step often causes frustration in the beginning. With practice it will get easier. The most important characteristic of the slipknot is that it is adjustable so it can be held snugly on your hook.

1 Leaving 6 to 8 inches at the end of your yarn, pinch the yarn between the thumb and pointer finger of your dominant hand.

2 Moving 3 to 4 inches along the yarn, pinch the yarn between the thumb and pointer finger of your other hand.

3 Bring your thumbs together. The yarn should twist into a loop.

4 Hold the loop closed with your non-dominant hand.

5 Bring the short end of the yarn behind the loop.

6 Grab the yarn that is crossing behind the loop with with your hook.

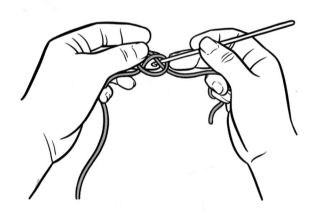

7 Carefully pull on both ends of the yarn until the slipknot forms around the hook. You should be able to adjust it to size by pulling on the short end.

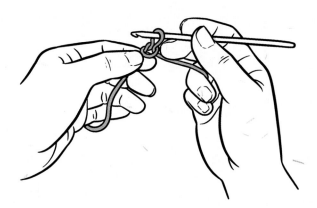

Stitch Height

The same foundation chain is made for all the basic stitches. The number of chains made will differ, though, due to the height difference of the stitch. The height of various stitches can be measured in chain lengths. The single crochet (Sc) will be the height of one chain, two chains for a half double crochet (Hdc), three for a double (Dc), and four for a triple (Trc). When working the foundation chain, extra chains are added to take this into account.

When working rows for which you turn and go back the other way or rounds that end with a slip stitch into the first stitch made, consideration must be given to the height of the next stitch planned. Some patterns use the chains to take the place of the first stitch. The pattern will read "Ch 3 counts as Dc." Other times when the chains are for height only, the pattern will read "Ch 2, Dc in same stitch."

When working in spirals, there is no need to chain at the end of rounds, but at the end of your work, you will need to "step down" to the round before so as not to leave a jagged edge. In order to step down from a Dc, place a Hdc in the next stitch, then a Sc in the next, and finally a Sl St in the next stitch, and the edge of your work will be smooth and ready for an edging such as the Rev Sc.

Stitch Placement and Combos

All the fancy crochet stitches are just the basic stitches worked in patterns. As long as you do not increase or decrease the number of stitches in a row, the stitches can be placed as desired.

For example, the V stitch is made by placing (Dc, Ch, Dc) all in the same stitch on the previous row. When that is done, the next two stitches must be skipped in order to maintain the same stitch count for the row. A shell is when multiple stitches are placed in the same stitch and then the appropriate number of stitches are skipped. When creating your own designs, it helps to draw a simple diagram using dots for the previous row and lines for the shell to make sure you can visualize the stitch count.

Textured stitches can be made in several ways. The popcorn and bobble stitches are made by removing the hook from the last stitch in a shell, inserting it into the first stitch and drawing the working loop through to bunch all the stitches together. A cluster is made by repeating the first steps of multiple stitches in the same stitch until desired loops are on the hook (similar to decreasing but done all in the same stitch). Then yarn over and pull through all the loops on the hook. Crocheting in the front or back posts of the rows below the working row will add texture similar to surface stitching. It will also allow your work to bend more easily. This is what is done in the case of adding a brim to a hat.

Tension

The amount of tension being applied to the yarn as we work determines the size of the stitches. The tension that individual crocheters can comfortably hold will vary. Regardless of these differences, the stitches should be uniform throughout the project. Most of the projects in this book do not rely on any particular size. If your poppet is a bit bigger than mine, no worries.

Meanwhile, I have made swatches using four-ply yarn and different size hooks. I have listed the measurements below. Do the same and you will get an idea of how our tension compares. You can then adjust the size hook used in my patterns or practice until your work matches mine.

Tension Swatch

To Begin: Ch 13, Hdc in third Ch from hook.

Row 1: *Hdc in first stitch, Hdc across (11), Ch 2, turn*

Row 2–6: Repeat between * *.

Swatch Measurements

J hook: 4" wide × 3.5" high
H hook: 3.5" wide × 3" high
F hook: 3" wide × 2.5" high

Stitch Markers

When working in rounds, it will be necessary to use a stitch marker to signify the end of each round. Move the marker up as you finish each round. There are markers available at the craft store, but I find a three-inch piece of yarn in a contrasting color works just as well.

Joining New Yarns

Somewhere along the way you will have to join two ends of yarn together. This may be because you need to change the color or because you need more yarn than one ball or skein contains. Either way you will want to do so as neatly as possible. These are the steps I take most often to accomplish this.

As you come to the last step of a stitch where the last two or three (in the case of a Hdc) loops are on the hook, lay the new color or additional yarn around the hook. Pull the new yarn through the loops of the stitch. Now continue with the pattern, working over the two ends. This will hide them nicely. Once you have crocheted over them for a few stitches to secure them, trim the ends.

Increasing and Decreasing

The rule of thumb to shaping is simple. In order to increase the size of your work, you need to add more stitches. Take some away in order to decrease the size of your piece. This is the way we make hats, bowls, goddesses, and so on. It's important to remember that when you are shaping, less is usually better than more. The row or round after the change in stitch count will expand or retract to the actual size. You do not even have to increase on every round, and you shouldn't unless you want a circle or sphere. Adding more stitches to every other round will give you a cone. The very best cone that I know of is . . . well, it's an ice cream cone, but second best is the basic witch's hat at the end of this chapter (see page 143).

Fiber Magick by the Numbers

There is a ton of counting involved in most thread and yarn work. This is part of the initial challenge folks have with crocheting. The rectangle quickly becomes a triangle if you are not making sure that the same number of stitches go into every row. "How do you know?" I have been asked. "You count them" is always my reply, oftentimes to the inquirer's great astonishment.

As you grow in your craft, you count less and "feel" more. When crocheting a shell stitch, for which you have to place five stitches in one so that it looks like a little fan, you just know when you have reached five. Partially because of muscle memory and partially because of the trance you have attained after making 5,000 shells. But either way, if you don't look down once in a while, you will find a four-stitch shell somewhere rows back. That's when we thank the Goddess for the magick of appliqué.

Honestly, I don't really mind the counting. I tend to count as I accomplish most tasks. It can be relaxing and keeps your mind focused on your work. This is perfect for when I'm crocheting magick. I consider what the numbers mean as I go to help set the intention. Including a bit of numerology into your Fiber Magick can be fun and useful. It gets us a step closer to actual spellwork.

Let's begin by assigning an attribute to each number:

0: Potential

1: Self-awareness

2: Balance, duality

3: Emphasis

4: Stability, grounding

5: Journeys, changes

6: Insight, clarity

7: Luck, chance

8: Success, abundance

9: Completion

10: Maturity

Think about the chakra anklet we made in chapter 4. We repeated nine chains three times. We were putting emphasis on the chakra that would complete our balance.

Combine the meanings to incorporate larger numbers. For instance, any of the teens brings that attribute into the self. All the twenty-somethings help with balancing the various attributes. I thought about zero for quite a while, and I think it can be used in your thought process each time you decrease a stitch. Continue to see the potential. This would make ten self-potential: bringing your potential around to yourself, also known as maturity.

You will also use more than one number when shaping. For instance, when making a bowl to throw your change in at the end of the day, start with rounds of four increases for stability, and then add a few rows of eight increases for success. You could then cause the bowl to cup inward by decreasing after every four stitches. Hold that potential stability in your mind! Seal the spell by doing a round of reverse crochet before you fasten off and weave in the ends. I see a very stable business venture in your future. May that spare change add up and bring you something wonderful.

Blocking

Blocking is an important step in finishing your work. As we crochet, we may find that our piece is not exactly in the shape we were going for. This can be especially true when we are making circles. Blocking will help.

Lay a piece of corrugated cardboard out onto a flat surface. Spread your crochet out onto the cardboard. Lightly spray the piece with water. Now you can pin the piece in place, sticking the pins directly into the cardboard, and allow to air dry.

Add a drop of essential oil to the water for an added correspondence.

Banish by Frogging

There will be times when we will need to let go of what no longer serves us to make room for new and better things. In crochet we call this *frogging* because you make like a frog and *rip it, rip it*. That's a bit of hooker humor. But seriously, when you compare the act of unraveling hard work because it is flawed somehow to banishing magick, you get a feel for the bittersweet emotions that can come with doing what you know to be right. Old habits and past relationships may have brought us a certain amount of joy at the time, but they are keeping us from moving forward. So they gotta go.

Crocheting a long chain while picturing your old self and then pulling the string and watching those chains disappear can be very cathartic. Add a few beads so that when you pull the string, the beads go flying in all directions. You can do this by finding beads with holes large enough for a small hook to go through. Yarn over and draw the yarn through the beads as you chain. When you pull the ends, watch as what those beads represent goes bouncing away from you. You do not even have to hunt them. Leave them for the vacuum cleaner.

Your Fiber Magick Journey

Whether or not you have crocheted before, Fiber Magick crochet needs to start at the very beginning. Ground and center, raise the energy, set the intention, and make that slipknot. Then practice chaining mindfully. Once you have the hang of it, add a few beads and make a wrap bracelet.

Clarity Bracelet

Set your mind for a positive experience and that's half the battle. The scent of rosemary to clear the mind and the color yellow to perk the intellect make an atmosphere conducive to learning new skills.

SKILL LEVEL
Beginner

FINISHED SIZE
24"

YOU WILL NEED
Lighter
Candle
1 drop of rosemary oil
3 yds of gray 4-ply
    yarn
Crochet hook size H/8
    5.00 mm
9 yellow pony beads

PREPARATION

Take 3 deep, cleansing breaths. Light the candle. Recite the Fiber Magick poem:

> A picture in the mind so clear
> It must travel down the artist's arm
> And come alive to greet the world
> As clothing fair or blanket warm.
> Hidden deep within the thread,
> Love so strong it will not fade.
> So much more is passed along
> When we give life to that handmade.

INSTRUCTIONS

1 Apply oil to the fingertips and run a foot or two of the yarn through your fingers. Breathe deeply and focus your intention into the yarn.

2 Thread the beads onto the yarn.

3 Leaving 6 inches from the end for tying, Ch 3.

4 Bring up a bead and Ch over it.

5 Ch 3, Ch over bead, Ch 3, Ch over bead, continuing until all beads are used, ending with Ch 3.

6 Wear it as a wrap bracelet or hang it on your altar as a witch's ladder.

7 Extinguish the candle.

Elemental Mojo Bag

This little bag uses all four of the stitches associated with the four elements as designated in the stitch guide at the beginning of this chapter. It makes a quick project to practice them all. Since the bag contains all the correspondences, you can make them in any color. I have several hanging above my candle-dressing station filled with spell components.

SKILL LEVEL
Beginner

FINISHED SIZE
4" × 4"

YOU WILL NEED
3 oz (156 yds) of 4-ply
  cotton yarn
Crochet hook size H/8
  5.00 mm
Scissors
Candle
Yarn needle

PREPARATION
Ground and center, light the candle, and recite this poem:

> Sweet magick I become,
> flesh and breath of dancing light.
> New wonders yet to come
> as I shine from day to night.
> Sweet magick I become,
> shedding all existing doubts.
> Free to open up my eyes
> and see what life is all about.

Imagine that dancing lights fill you up and come to rest in your hands.

INSTRUCTIONS

Ch 17.

Row 1 Sl St in each Ch across, corresponding to earth, Ch 1, and turn (16).

Row 2 Sc in each stitch across, corresponding to water, Ch 1, and turn (16).

Row 3 Hdc in each stitch across, corresponding to fire, Ch 2, and turn (16).

Row 4 Dc in each stitch across, corresponding to air, Ch 2, and turn (16).

Row 5 Hdc in each stitch across, corresponding to fire, Ch 1, and turn (16).

Row 6 Sc in each stitch across, corresponding to water, Ch 1, and turn (16).

Row 7 Sl St in each stitch across, corresponding to earth, Ch 1, and turn (16).

Fold the piece in half. Working through both thicknesses, Sc around 3 sides, leaving an opening at the top. Put 2 Sc in each corner to turn.

Sc around the opening. Sl St into first Sc.

Ch 12 and Sl St in the same corner, or make the chain long enough to use as a necklace and Sl St in the opposite corner.

Bless your work and extinguish the candle.

Herbal Blends for Mojo Bags

Make these bags in the appropriate color, embroider them with the proper sigil, and fill them with an herbal blend to attract the desired results.

INTENTION	HERBS	COLOR AND SIGIL
Health	Cedar, cinnamon, eucalyptus	Place in a green or blue bag with a leaf sigil
Love	Lemon balm, basil, cardamom, vanilla	Place in a red or pink bag with a heart sigil
Luck	Bamboo, catnip, cotton	Place in a light blue or green bag with a smiley face sigil
Money	Allspice, bergamot, buckwheat	Place in a green bag with a money sigil
Peace	Anise seed, chamomile, gardenia	Place in a pink or white bag with a peace sigil
Protection	Carnation, clove, rosemary	Place in a black bag with a shield sigil
Psychic ability	Bay, flax, mugwort, hemp	Place in a purple bag with a third eye sigil

Crochet with Intent

When we perform a fiber art such as crochet, we are literally making hundreds of knots. The correlation between this and knot magick is clear. All we need to add is intention. With every stitch, we can build the energy needed to bring healing, comfort, or protection. This is recognized by even the most mainstream spiritualities.

For instance, a prayer shawl is a shawl that has been made while the Fiber Magick practitioner was praying. The prayer shawl holds the healing energy to be wrapped around the infirm like loving arms. There can be a ritual upon completion to dedicate a shawl to a particular person. With this practice, the crafter could make shawls when they can, to be used when needed. Even without a personal dedication, the shawl could still be filled with hope for the greater good. In this way, the shawl can live on to comfort others after the original owner has no further need of it.

In Fiber Magick, it is important to understand that it is not always our beliefs that will do the healing. It will be the beliefs of the recipient that matter, even though they may be different from ours. Once, I made a shawl with the word *believe* crocheted into it. This one went to a woman who had broken her back. She was told that it was not likely that she would ever regain her mobility. I asked her to wrap herself in her belief that she would walk again. Guess what? Yep! She now walks. I have no doubt it was her determination and belief in herself that made it possible.

There are several shawls still in hospice that I have made. These were ones I made for my husband's grandmother. One has the initials GG on it. Those initials are not for her name but for her title, great grandma. Rest assured they deliver comfort where it is needed. It will find its way to other GGs. The energy knows and can adapt to the individual's religious beliefs.

There may be times when the shawl is not meant to be shared. One in particular was made for a woman who was very ill and knew she would never see her homeland again. Her nephew had me crochet a lapghan for her in the colors of her country's flag. I was told she grabbed on to it and did not let go. Eventually, she was laid to rest with it. I believe it gave her family as much comfort as it did her.

When making any prayer shawl, prepare yourself with breath work, poetry, and the right cup of tea in order to put all the healing you can into it.

Simple Prayer Shawl

- -

For this shawl we will be making a mesh fabric. Place all Dc in the corresponding Dc on the previous row with a Ch 1 between them.

Beginning V Stitch (Beg V St): Ch 4 (counts as Dc, Ch 1) + Dc in same stitch

V Stitch (V St): Dc + Ch 1 + Dc in same stitch

SKILL LEVEL
Intermediate

FINISHED SIZE
76" × 42"

YOU WILL NEED
16 oz (832 yds) of 4-ply yarn
Crochet hook size J/10 6.00 mm

PREPARATION: BANISH ANY STRESS

1 Ch 7 while focusing any stress into the yarn.

2 Hold each end and pull.

3 Watch the stress go *poof* as the chains disappear.

INSTRUCTIONS

Start at the bottom tip of the shawl.

Row 1 Ch 4 (counts as Dc + Ch 1), Dc in fourth Ch from hook, turn.

Row 2 Beg V St, V St in next Dc, turn.

Row 3 Beg V St, {Ch 1, Dc, Ch 1} across V St in third Ch of Beg V St on previous row, turn. Repeat row 3 until shawl is desired size. End with an odd number of rows to add the shell border.

SHELL BORDER

1 Working down the side, Ch 1 and place 7 Dc in top of Ch 3 of previous row, {1 Sc in top of first stitch on next row down, 5 Dc in top of first stitch on next row down} until second to last row.

2 Space 7 Sc evenly around the tip of the shawl.

Adding a blessing at the end of a project is always a good practice, even more so when the item is meant as a gift of healing. Ask your deities or, better yet, the deities of the recipient to oversee the desired effect. This is the place where folk medicine and folk magick meet. Always bless an item from a place of love and gratitude.

3 {5 Dc in top of first stitch on next row down, 1 Sc in top of first stitch on next row down} up other side, place 7 Dc in top of first stitch on second to last row, Ch 1 and Sl St into top of first stitch on last row.

4 Fasten off and weave in the ends.

5 Bless your finished prayer shawl and gift it to someone in need.

PRAYER SHAWL BLESSING

Perform the project blessing ritual on page 17 and declare,

> *This shawl will wrap (person's name) in healing light and love! So mote it be.*

Crocheted Circle

Crocheting a circle involves working in rounds instead of rows. The geometry of a circle calls for the circumference to grow along with the diameter. Increasing the stitch count consistently on every round allows for the circle to remain flat until the increasing stops and the work begins to form a cup. When a circle larger than four or five rounds is needed, staggering the placement of the increases helps keep the shape nice and round. Use a stitch marker and move it up at the end of every round.

SKILL LEVEL
Beginner

FINISHED SIZE
4" diameter

YOU WILL NEED
1 oz (52 yds) of 4-ply
   yarn
Crochet hook size H/8
   5.00 mm
Stitch marker to
   designate the end of
   your rounds

INSTRUCTIONS

Ch 2.

Rd 1 6 Sc in second Ch from hook (6).

Rd 2 2 Sc in each stitch around (12).

Rd 3 {1 Sc, 2 Sc} around (18).

Rd 4 {1 Sc twice, 2 Sc} around (24).

Rd 5 Rev Sc in each stitch around (24).

Candle Cozy

- -

This cozy acts as instant candle dressing and makes an ordinary 7-day candle into a Fiber Magick candle. Inexpensive white candles can be transformed into whatever you need them to be. The Hdc adds the element of fire. Use cotton yarn to avoid the acrylic type melting.

SKILL LEVEL
Beginner

FINISHED SIZE
Fits a 7-day candle

YOU WILL NEED
4 oz (208 yds) of
   cotton yarn
Stitch marker
7-day candle

PREPARATION

Take 3 deep breaths and Ch 7, filling them with any negativity you may be feeling. Hold both ends and pull. Light the candle and recite this poem:

> *Blessed Minerva, Great Goddess of Crafts,*
> *Who helps us to conjure the world with our hands,*
> *To take the mundane with its worry and strife,*
> *To weave in the magick and bring it to life.*

INSTRUCTIONS

Ch 2.

Rd 1 6 Sc in second Ch from hook (6).

Rd 2 2 Sc in each stitch around (12).

Rd 3 {2 Sc, 1 Sc} around (18).

Rd 4 {2 Sc, 1 Sc twice} around (24). Sl St in next stitch.

Rd 5 Ch 1, Hdc in back loops only around, Sl St in first Hdc (24).

Rd 6–16 Ch 1, Hdc in each stitch around, Sl St in first Hdc (24).

Rd 17 Sl St into next St, Rev Sc around (24).

Fasten off and weave in the ends.

Crocheted Mandala

- -

The crocheted mandala pattern calls for you to Sl St at the end of each round instead of working into the next stitch like for a spiral. You have a choice at that time to either continue by chaining to start the next round or to cut your yarn, fasten off (pulling the end of the yarn through the loop to make a knot), and attach a new color with a slip stitch. Once your mandala is done, you can use it as a meditation tool to bring you back to the Divine, where you started.

SKILL LEVEL
Intermediate

FINISHED SIZE
24"

YOU WILL NEED
About 16 oz (832 yds) of 4-ply yarn in a variety of colors
24" hula-hoop
Crochet hook size H/8 5.00 mm

INSTRUCTIONS

Rd 1 Ch 6 and Sl St into first Ch made to form ring.

Rd 2 Ch 3 (counts as Dc), make 11 Dc in ring, Sl St in top of Ch 3.

Rd 3 Ch 4 (counts as Dc + Ch 1), Dc + Ch 1 in each stitch around, Sl St in third Ch of Ch 4.

Rd 4 Sl St into next Ch Sp, Ch 4 (counts as Dc + Ch 1) + Dc in same space, Dc + Ch 1 + Dc (V St) in every Ch Sp around, Sl St in third Ch of Ch 4.

Rd 5 Sl St into next V St, Ch 3 (counts as Dc) + 4 Dc in same V St, 5 Dc in each V St around (5 Dc shell), Sl St in top of Ch 3.

Rd 6 Ch 3 (counts as Dc) + 5 Dc in same space between shells, 6 Dc in each space between shells around, Sl St in top of Ch 3.

Rd 7 Ch 3 (counts as Dc) + 3 Dc in same space between shells, {skip next 3 Dc and V St between Dcs in center of 6 Dc shell, skip next 3 Dc and 4 Dc shell between shells} around, Sl St in top of Ch 3.

Rd 8 Sl St to center of 4 Dc shell, Ch 3 (counts as Dc) + 6 Dc in same space, {Sc in next V St, 7 Dc shell in center of next 4 Dc shell} around, Sl St in top of Ch 3.

Rd 9 Sl St in next 2 Dc, Ch 1 and Sc in same stitch, Sc in next 2 stitches, 2 Dc + Ch 2 + 2 Dc in next Sc, {skip 2 Dc, Sc in next 3 stitches, 2 Dc + Ch 2 + 2 Dc in next Sc} around, Sl St in first Sc.

Rd 10 Sl St into next Sc, Ch 3 (counts as Dc) + Dc + Ch 1 + 2 Dc in same stitch, {2 Dc + Ch 1 + 2 Dc in Ch Sp of next shell, 2 Dc + Ch 1 + 2 Dc in center Sc in next 3 Sc group} around, Sl St into top of Ch 3.

Rd 11 Ch 3 (counts as Dc), Dc in each of next 9 stitches (Dcs and Ch Sps), {Ch 1, Dc in each of next 10 stitches} around, Sl St in top of Ch 3.

Rd 12 Ch 3 (counts as Dc), Dc in each of next 9 stitches, {2 Dc in Ch Sp, Dc in each of next 10 stitches} around, Sl St in top of Ch 3.

Rd 13 Ch 3 (counts as Dc) + Dc + Ch 2 + 2 Dc in same stitch, skip next 5 stitches, 7 Dc shell in next stitch, {skip next 5 stitches, 2 Dc + Ch 2 + 2 Dc in next stitch, skip next 5 stitches, 7 Dc shell in next stitch} around, Sl St in top of Ch 3.

Rd 14 Sl St to next Ch space, Ch 3 (counts as Dc) + 6 Dc in same Ch Sp, {7 Dc shell in center stitch of next 7 Dc shell, 7 Dc shell in next Ch Sp} around, Sl St in top of Ch 3.

Rd 15 Ch 3 (counts as Dc), Dc in each of next 13 stitches (Dcs and Ch Sps), {Ch 1, Dc in each of next 14 stitches} around, Sl St in top of Ch 3.

Rd 16 Ch 3 (counts as Dc), Dc in each of next 13 stitches, {2 Dc in Ch Sp, Dc in each of next 14 stitches} around, Sl St in top of Ch 3.

Rd 17 Ch 1, 2 Sc in same stitch working over the hula-hoop, 2 Sc in each stitch around and working over the hula-hoop. Sl St in first Sc.

Ch 20, Sl St in same stitch to form loop for hanging.

Fasten off and work in any ends.

Drawstring Magickal Bag

In this example the pattern begins with each round increasing by six stitches. This pouch could be said to contain the energy of the number six. I have assigned the correspondences of insight and clarity to the number six. The double crochet stitches add the element of air and the correspondence of the intellect. Storing runes in a bag like this could increase the power of divination.

SKILL LEVEL
Beginner

FINISHED SIZE
8"

YOU WILL NEED
6 oz (312 yds) of 4-ply
  yarn
Crochet hook size I/9
  5.50 mm
Stitch marker

INSTRUCTIONS

Ch 3.

Rd 1 6 Dc on third Ch from hook (6).

Rd 2 2 Dc in each stitch around (12).

Rd 3 {1 Dc, 2 Dc} around (18).

Rd 4 {1 Dc twice, 2 Dc} around (24).

Rd 5 {1 Dc 3 times, 2 Dc} around (30).

Rd 6 {1 Dc 4 times, 2 Dc} around (36).

Rd 7–9 1 Dc in each stitch around (36).

Step down from the spiral by making a Hdc, Sc, and Sl St.

Rd 10 Ch 4, skip next stitch, {Dc in next stitch, skip next stitch, Ch 1} around, Sl St in top of Ch 3.

Rd 11 Ch 2, 2 Hdc in each Ch Sp around, Sl St in first Hdc.

Rd 12 Ch 1, Rev Sc around.

Fasten off.

THE DRAW STRING

Ch 60, fasten off, and weave through the Ch Sps on Rd 10.

You could also make this pouch using multiples of other numbers. Start with 7 Dc in first stitch from hook. Follow the same pattern but with an increase of the number seven in each round and store your gaming dice in a pouch infused with luck. Now you're rolling 20.

Wish Bowl

I developed these tiny wish bowls for a psychic fair. It went over pretty well. People seemed to enjoy creating their own reading. They loved the fact that they had a token to take home and remind them of the insight they received. When making a wish bowl for someone else, my advice is to keep it simple. Although no one seemed to mind that I had all the charts spread out on my table. Maybe they didn't know I can read upside down and backward.

There's no reason why you can't make one for yourself. Just try not to overthink it when it comes to the choosing of the colors, herbs, and oils. If you are forgetful like me and don't have all the correspondences memorized, it may make for a surprising outcome. Choose all your materials without thinking about it too much and then see what the universe wants you to realize. You don't have to be a super psychic or medium to make wish bowls. Wish bowls are a discipline that allows a person to really think about what they want. They are a systematic focus on the situation. They might even help you change your mind, and that is the very first step to changing anything.

SKILL LEVEL
Intermediate

FINISHED SIZE
3" diameter

YOU WILL NEED
Yarn in an assortment
  of colors
Various oils
Collection of herbs
Stone or crystal beads
Crochet size H/8
  5.00 mm
Needle
Thread
Correspondence lists of
  those herbs, beads,
  and oils

PREPARATION

1 Arrange the yarns, oils, and herbs on the table in front of you.

2 Close your eyes and take three deep, cleansing breaths. As you breathe slowly in and out, think about what you want to wish for. Be specific and really picture this thing actually manifesting.

3 When you open your eyes, choose the color yarn, the oil, the herb, and the bead that speaks to you. Place those four things in a row in front of you.

4 Bring awareness to the color of yarn. Consider the meanings.

INSTRUCTIONS

Ch 3. As you do, call upon the Triple Goddess for insight:

Maiden, Mother, Crone.

Rd 1 12 Dc in third Ch from hook (12).

Consider the number twelve and its meaning. You can do the math as you see fit: 1 + 2 = self-balance, or 4 × 3 = emphasis on stability. Play with the combinations.

Rub this little circle with the herb. As you do, think about what correspondence that adds to your wish. Is it something you need to do before this wish can manifest? Try to be honest with yourself.

Rd 2 {2 Dc, 1 Dc} around (18).

You are adding six for insight. You could also do some more math: 1 + 8 = self-success, and 3 × 6 = triple insight.

Time to add the bead. While sewing the bead into the bottom of your bowl, think about its properties and how it might relate to your wish.

Rd 3 {1 Dc, 2 Dc Tog} around (12).

Balance your success as you decrease from 18 stitches to 12.

Anoint the rim of the bowl with a drop of the oil, adding the next layer of intention as you do. Take another deep breath here. How do the aromas of the herb and oil working together make you feel? Are you satisfied with this wish? Do you want it to manifest?

Rd 4 Rev Sc around.

Fasten off and weave in the ends. When making this for someone else, have them cut the yarn and weave in the ends to symbolize them taking action and making this wish their goal.

Add a blessing:

Goddess wise and generous true,
I made this bowl as a wish to you.
Please see it manifest as such,
And I praise and thank you very much.
So mote it be.

USE

Place your little wish bowl on your altar or nightstand to remind you of what you need to do to attain that wish. Wishing and hoping is all very good, but your intention will never manifest without action.

I have even made a little bowl like this for someone who was going through hard times. Using black yarn, black pepper, cloves, obsidian, and the like will make a little black hole for negativity. Place this beside your bed and give it the day's stresses to get a good night's sleep. A spritz of lavender on your pillow would be nice as well.

Witch's Hat

- -

The hat is made by holding two strands of four-ply yarn together. The strands can be the same color to make a solid color hat or two complementary colors to make a sort of tweed look. Some winning combinations have been black and any other color but mostly gray or purple.

Hold the tension firmly when crocheting so the hat stands up and can be shaped. If you find it hard to hold a firm tension, just use a smaller hook. Your tension and your head size will tell you if you need to increase again or stop earlier. The kids may want one too. This hat can be made as tall as you like, but it may flop over and become a gnome's hat. For a gnome's hat, you may want to make a narrower brim or roll it up wizard style.

Mark the rounds as you go. This becomes a true blessing when you get up into the bigger rounds. Repeat patterns between { } until you get back to your marker.

SKILL LEVEL
Intermediate

FINISHED SIZE
Adjustable

YOU WILL NEED
Crochet hook size H/8 5.00 mm or hook needed for gauge
2 7-oz skeins (364 yds each) of 4-ply yarn in desired colors
Stitch marker
Yarn needle

INSTRUCTIONS

Ch 2 and 6 Hdc in second Ch from hook.

Rd 1 (In FLO) 1 Hdc in each stitch around (6).

Turn the tip right-side out. This will give you a pointier tip to your hat.

Rd 2 {2 Hdc, 1 Hdc} around (9).

Rd 3 1 Hdc in each stitch around (9).

Rd 4 {2 Hdc, 1 Hdc twice} around (12).

Rd 5 1 Hdc in each stitch around (12).

Rd 6 {2 Hdc, 1 Hdc twice} around (16).

Rd 7 1 Hdc in each stitch around (16).

Rd 8 {2 Hdc, 1 Hdc 3 times} around (20).

Rd 9 1 Hdc in each stitch around (20).

Rd 10 {2 Hdc, 1 Hdc 3 times} around (25).

Rd 11 1 Hdc in each stitch around (25).

Rd 12 {2 Hdc, 1 Hdc 4 times} around (30).

Rd 13 1 Hdc in each stitch around (30).

Rd 14 {2 Hdc, 1 Hdc 4 times} around (36).

Rd 15 1 Hdc in each stitch around (36).

Rd 16 {2 Hdc, 1 Hdc 5 times} around (42).

Rd 17 1 Hdc in each stitch around (42).

Rd 18 {2 Hdc, 1 Hdc 5 times} around (49).

Rd 19 1 Hdc in each stitch around (49).

Rd 20 {2 Hdc, 1 Hdc 6 times} around (56).

Rd 21 1 Hdc in each stitch around (56).

Rd 22 {2 Hdc, 1 Hdc 6 times} around (64).

Rd 23 1 Hdc in each stitch around (64).

FOR A SMALLER HAT

Rd 24–30 1 Hdc in each stitch around (64).

Continue with brim.

FOR A LARGER HAT

Rd 24 {2 Hdc, 1 Hdc 7 times} around (72).

Rd 25–32 1 Hdc in each stitch around (72).

BRIM

1 Sc in next stitch, 1 Sl St in next stitch, Ch 1, turn.

Working in BLO:

Rd 1 {2 Hdc, 1 Hdc 4 times} around.

Join with Sl St in first Hdc made at the end of each round, Ch 1, turn.

Continue in both loops.

Rd 2 1 Hdc in each stitch around, join with Sl St, Ch 1, turn.

Rd 3 {2 Hdc, 1 Hdc 4 times} around, join with Sl St, Ch 1, turn.

Rd 4 1 Hdc in each stitch around, join with Sl St, Ch 1, turn.

Rd 5 {2 Hdc, 1 Hdc 4 times} around, join with Sl St, Ch 1, turn.

Rd 6 1 Hdc in each stitch around, join with Sl St, Ch 1.

Rd 7 Rev Sc in each stitch around.

Fasten off and weave in the ends.

Time now to block and embellish. This is where the basic hat becomes fabulous. If you have kept the tension firm, your hat should be shapeable. Pull and twist it into your idea of a witch's chapeau. Go ahead. You won't break it.

You may want to add a hat band. Find a wide ribbon or use a scarf. You can also crochet one.

HATBAND

1 Ch 7.

2 For the first row, 1 Hdc in second Ch from hook, 1 Hdc in each stitch across (6).

3 All further rows Ch 1, 1 Hdc in BLO in each stitch across (6).

4 Continue until the band is long enough to encircle your hat just above the brim. No matter what you use for a band, you should tack it in place with a few stitches all the way around and then go on to further embellishment.

EMBELLISHMENT

Add a feather or any of the crocheted sigils that you will find in chapter 9. Hang a charm or two from the tip. In other words, allow Spirit to move you and make it your own. This is your time to shine creatively.

The hat chosen for the cover of this book was a hat I made some years ago. The feather that embellishes it is a pattern that is easily found on the internet from multiple sources. Although I won't share the exact pattern with you here, I would like to explain the meditative properties I find in a pattern such as this.

The pattern calls for an increase of stitches on the ends of the rows and an equal decrease as you reach the center. The triple front post stitch in the very center dips down into the previous row. This pattern can be continued for as long as you wish, determining the length of the feather. Then the increases and decreases decline, creating a tip.

As you perform the steps, think about adding a positive aspect to the feather while increasing, then removing a negative as you decrease. Mentally expand and contract, breathe in and out, go with the flow, and ground at center when you place the triple crochet.

Chapter 8

Advanced Fiber Magick Crochet: Poppets

When I was in the fourth grade, the art teacher at Park Elementary was awesome. She wore clam diggers and T-shirts when all the other female teachers wore dresses. She was always covered in paint or clay and wore very sensible shoes. She arrived in the classroom on her assigned days with a trolley of craft supplies and a tall stack of newspapers to cover our desks.

On one occasion she had us making papier-mâché puppets. Unfortunately, I accidentally made the nose on my puppet too big. It was the butt of all the jokes until she came over, gave it a good inspection, and proclaimed it to be Ringo Starr. Then, everyone loved it. Some kids wanted to trade theirs for mine. Nope. I kept my big-nosed puppet head and gave it a Beatles haircut of black paint. I wish I had a picture of it.

That will always stand out to me as being one of the worst times (being made fun of) and one of the best times (being vindicated) of my childhood. I felt triumphant. I guess I got a small taste of how Rudolph the Red-Nosed Reindeer must have felt. It also stands out to me now because it was my first experience with a poppet, although I had no idea that was what I was doing at that time. Regardless, it was magickal!

Now that you have tried your hand at shaping, increasing, decreasing, and the like, you are ready to tackle the doll-making portion of Fiber Magick. Your healing and protection work will explode with the use of the poppet.

The Ethics of Poppets

The most popular misconception about poppets is that they are always made to exact revenge against enemies or control someone's actions. These dolls can actually be used to represent a person for the purpose of sending them healing. Any tool used for magickal purposes can be charged to possess positive or negative vibrations through ceremony or meditation. The poppet is a tool just like a hammer. You can use a hammer to build a house or to knock it down. And, sometimes, just like when you are remodeling a kitchen, you have to knock it down before you can build it back up. Intention makes it harmful or helpful.

While these poppets can be used for harmful purposes, it is always in our best interest to strive to harm none. It is always best to communicate with the recipient of your healing. Magick should never be practiced on a person without their consent.

Stuffing and 3D Work

A note about stuffing if I may: always stuff as you go. Don't wait too long or you won't be able to get down into those little nooks and crannies. Add small amounts of stuffing at a time. You get better control that way and avoid bulges. You will also want to shape your poppet as you stuff. A squeeze here and there will get the stuffing where it needs to be. Stuff firmly but do not overdo it. You should not be seeing the stuffing through the stitches. If the stitches are a little too large in places, thread the same yarn on a large needle and darn it. Be gentle so as not to pull more holes than you started with. Maybe you could use a different color yarn and add some character to your poppet. It will look like a well-loved poppet indeed.

Poppets usually contain magickal components such as herbs, oils, crystals, and even fingernails and hair, as fitting the spell or action associated with them. These components should be added to the stuffing. This way the bits of herbs and crystal chips are less likely to work themselves out through the stitches.

Flatten out a handful of fluff, sprinkle with the desired additives, and roll it up like a burrito. Knead it a bit to get it all incorporated, and then stuff as usual.

Cleansing, Storing, and Destroying

In the case of healing spells and rituals, there is no need to destroy the poppet each time. It can be cleansed by giving it a nice rub down with salt and passing it through some sage smoke. It will be good as new and ready to send more healing where needed. Store the poppet in a bag or box with a piece of selenite to keep it company. The selenite will keep it clean with its strong positive energy.

If you need to destroy the poppet, such as in the case of a banishing or binding work, make sure you use a natural yarn like cotton. Cotton is safe to burn or bury in the ground.

Advanced Fiber Magick Crochet: Poppets

Crocheted Poppet

- -

Your doll can be adorned with items of clothing, jewelry, charms, and so on that hold meaning for the person you are making it for. Although not exact, you can suggest the hair color of that person with red, yellow, brown, or black yarn. In this way, you are connecting this doll to that person and directly sending them the healing they have requested.

SKILL LEVEL
Intermediate

FINISHED SIZE
8"

YOU WILL NEED
Stitch marker
4 oz (208 yds) of 4-ply yarn
Crochet hook size H/8 5.00 mm
1 button
Small amounts of black yarn and red embroidery floss for features
Stuffing with magickal components
Yarn needle

INSTRUCTIONS
Working in rounds, move the stitch marker up at the end of each round.

HEAD AND BODY

Ch 2.

Rd 1 6 Sc in second Ch from hook (6).

Rd 2 2 Sc in each stitch around (12).

Rd 3 {1 Sc, 2 Sc} around (18).

Rd 4 {2 Sc, 1 Sc twice} around (24).

Rd 5–7 1 Sc in each stitch around (24).

Rd 8 {2 Sc Tog, 1 Sc twice} around (18).

Rd 9 {1 Sc, 2 Sc Tog} around (12).

Rd 10 1 Sc in each stitch around (12).

Rd 11 2 Sc in each stitch around (24).

Rd 12 1 Sc in each stitch around (24).

Now is a good time to stuff the head.

Rd 13 {2 Sc, 1 Sc twice} around (32).

Rd 14–19 1 Sc in each stitch around (32).

Stuff as you go and add any herbs, crystals, charms, and so on that you care to add. More goodies can be added when stuffing the arms and legs. You can spread it around.

Rd 20 {2 Sc Tog, 1 Sc twice} around (24).

Rd 21 {1 Sc, 2 Sc Tog} around (16).

Rd 22 2 Sc Tog around (8).

Finish stuffing a bit more if necessary.

Sl St in next stitch. Fasten off. Leave a tail long enough to weave through and tighten the 8 remaining stitches. Tie off and hide the end by pulling it up into the doll.

ARMS AND LEGS (MAKE 4)

Ch 2.

Rd 1 6 Sc in second Ch from hook (6).

Rd 2 2 Sc in each stitch around (12).

Rd 3–8 1 Sc in each stitch around (12).

Sl St in next stitch. Fasten off and leave a tail for sewing. Stuff, sew closed, then sew to body.

DECORATING

Sew on a button for one eye and make an X for the other.

The mouth can be a smile or a straight line with cross stitches.

Embroider a heart shape on its chest with red floss.

Cut 3 short pieces of black yarn. Fold them in half and hook them onto the top of the head with a lark's head knot to make hair.

USING YOUR POPPET

Your poppet is now ready to be used to send energy out to where it is needed. Write down what you would like to see happen on a small slip of paper. Place the paper under your poppet and lean the poppet up against a 7-day candle. Light the candle. Send your light, love, and healing energies out to the person in need, and leave it to your poppet to continue that for you. When the candle has burned out, burn the paper as well. It is done.

Goddess of Journeys

This poppet is actually two godesses in one. The Roman goddess Abeona will see you off on your journey into the world, and her partner Adiona will see you safely home. This could be an actual trip or your path in general.

When you are physically traveling, keep this poppet with you in your bag or set it up on the dashboard for a calm, safe trip. If she is guarding your spiritual path, make her a place on your altar. Either way, increases in multiples of five and the calming scent of lavender will make for a pleasant journey.

SKILL LEVEL
Intermediate

FINISHED SIZE
8"

YOU WILL NEED
Candle
1 tsp of lavender for a
    calm journey
Fiberfill for stuffing
4 oz (208 yds) of 4-ply
    yarn
Crochet hook size H/8
    5.00 mm
Stitch marker

PREPARATION

1 Take three deep breaths.

2 Light the candle.

3 Meditate for a moment on your trip or path.

4 Add lavender to a handful of the stuffing.

INSTRUCTIONS

Ch 2.

Rd 1 5 Hdc in second Ch from hook.

Rd 2 1 Hdc in each stitch around (5).

Rd 3 2 Hdc in each stitch around (10).

Rd 4 1 Hdc in each stitch around (10).

Rd 5 {2 Hdc, 1 Hdc} around (15).

Rd 6 1 Hdc in each stitch around (15).

Rd 7 {1 Hdc twice, 2 Hdc} around (20).

Rd 8 1 Hdc in each stitch around (20).

Rd 9 {1 Hdc 3 times, 2 Hdc} around (25).

Rd 10–14 1 Hdc in each stitch around (25).

Stuff the body with lavender fluff.

Rd 15 2 Sc Tog around until 12 stitches are left (12).

Rd 16–17 Sc in each stitch around (12).

Rd 18 {2 Hdc twice, 1 Hdc} around (20).

Rd 19–21 1 Hdc in each stitch around (20).

Rd 22 2 Sc Tog around (10).

Finish stuffing.

Rd 23 2 Sc Tog around (5).

Cut the yarn, weave the end through the remaining 5 stitches, and pull to close. Draw the end into the doll.

ARMS

1 Attach the yarn to the side of the body above round 12.

2 Ch 10, Sc in top of head, Ch 10, Sl St in opposite side of body above round 12.

3 Ch 1, turn, evenly space 15 Dc on Ch 10.

4 Put 5 Dc in Sc on top of head.

5 Evenly space 15 Dc on Ch 10 on opposite side of body.

6 Sl St into round 12.

7 Fasten off, leaving ends free to use in blessing.

BLESSING FOR A GODDESS OF JOURNEYS

Knot the ends and pull them into the body as you chant,

> *Goddess of Journeys, guard my way.*
> *See that my travels to the end*
> *Are good and sound and meaningful.*
> *Then bring me safely back again.*
> *So mote it be.*

Chakra Healing with a Poppet

When you are doing long-distance healing, it is very useful to have a focus. A poppet lets you imagine the area of the body being treated. This is the job of the chakra doll. It is about the length of an average forearm and relatively flat, so it nestles nicely between your arms. There are colorful circles on the front that act as pockets for your crystals or charms. An upbuilding note of encouragement could be tucked into the chakra in need of a boost.

When choosing the color of your doll, keep it neutral so that the emphasis will be on the chakra discs. White can take the place of any color. Beige is easier to keep looking clean. Gray brings out the true color of the other colors.

Chakra Doll with Pockets

- -

The dominant Fiber Magick number in the chakra doll pattern is 8. The legs and arms start with 8 stitches and then double. The body jumps to 5 × 8, or 40. So the number 8 corresponds with success and 5 for journeys. In long-distance healing you are taking the healing energy into yourself and sending it out on a journey to where it is needed. Success!

SKILL LEVEL
Advanced

FINISHED SIZE
16"

YOU WILL NEED
Crochet hook size H/8
    5.00 mm
7 oz (364 yds) of yarn
    in a neutral color
Stitch marker
4 yds of yarn in each
    of the chakra colors:
    red, orange, yellow,
    green, blue, purple,
    and violet
Yarn needle

ARMS AND LEGS (MAKE 4)

Ch 2.

Rd 1 8 Hdc in second Ch from hook (8).

Rd 2 2 Hdc in each stitch around (16).

Rd 3–13 1 Hdc in each stitch around (16).

Sc in next stitch, Sl St in next stitch, fasten off for first 3. Do not fasten off the fourth.

Hold two of the pieces together to form the legs, and connect them with 3 Sl St.

BODY

Ch 1.

Rd 1 {2 Hdc, 1 Hdc 3 times} around (40).

Make sure you get in the Sl St front and back. You will know you have it when you have 40 stitches around.

Lightly stuff the legs at this time. You want the doll to be flat so you can hold it between your forearms and connect with the chakras. Do not over stuff.

Rd 2–16 1 Hdc in each stitch around (40).

It is important to use your stitch marker for these rounds to get proper shoulder placement. After 16

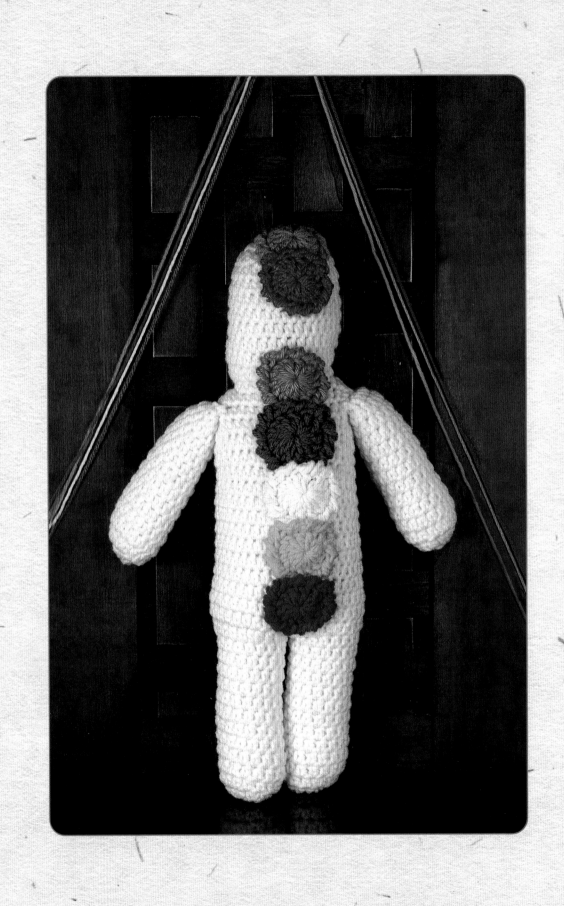

rounds of 40 stitches, you will be ready to do a 5-stitch decrease. To do this, Yo, insert hook in next stitch, Yo, and pull through 2 loops in the next 5 stitches. There should be 6 loops on your hook. Yo and pull through all 6 stitches.

Lightly stuff the body as you go, also making sure the doll remains flat.

SHOULDERS, NECK, AND HEAD

Rd 1 5 Hdc Tog, 1 Hdc 15 times, 5 Hdc Tog, 1 Hdc 14 times (32).

Rd 2 5 Hdc Tog, 1 Hdc 11 times, 5 Hdc Tog, 1 Hdc 10 times (24).

Rd 3 1 Hdc in each stitch around (24).

Rd 4 1 Hdc twice, 5 Hdc in next stitch, 1 Hdc 11 times, 5 Hdc in next St, 1 Hdc 9 times (32).

Rd 5–11 1 Hdc in each stitch around (32).

Rd 12 {2 Hdc Tog, 1 Hdc} around (21).

Rd 13 2 Hdc Tog 13 times, 2 Sc Tog, Sl St (8).

Finish stuffing.

Fasten off, leaving long tail for sewing. Weave it through the last 8 stitches and pull tight. Secure and hide the end.

Stuff lightly and attach the arms just under the shoulders.

CHAKRA CIRCLES

1 Ch 4.

2 12 Dc in third chain from hook.

3 Sl St in top of Ch 4 (13).

4 Rev Sc around.

5 Fasten off, leaving long tail for sewing.

6 Sew the circles over the chakra points along the body, leaving the top of each circle open to act as a pocket for crystals and herbs. Working downward, start at the crown and overlap the circles just a bit in order to get proper placement and illustrate how each chakra moves into the next.

Advanced Fiber Magick Crochet: Poppets

A Fascination with Mermaids

I have a friend who loves mermaids. She is usually wearing some piece of jewelry or clothing that reflects this obsession. She collects mermaid everything and vends at nautical craft shows. Basically, she is a mermaid. I can dig it. The ocean and all its mysteries seem so close and yet so far away. It's easy to imagine freedom and a carefree life among the waves. We can ignore the potential dangers in our mind's eye. Ah, perception—so much more important than reality.

Most every culture has legends of water creatures and spirits. Undines, krakens, and merfolk adorn the cave walls and embellish seafarers' stories. These stories go from joyous to horrifying, but all of them are surreal. As Pagans, we might call some of these creatures and spirits to join us in ritual. We invite them from the west to add the element of water to our rite. They represent the emotional parts of us. The water of the Mother's womb washes over us and heals us. For a moment, in the moment, we return to our original home. In our biological mother's womb, we were all once merfolk.

Mermaid Poppet

The mermaid will make an excellent addition to a west altar.

SKILL LEVEL
Advanced

FINISHED SIZE
20"

YOU WILL NEED
Crochet hook size H/8
   5.00 mm
4 oz (208 yds) of 4-ply
   yarn in a color of
   your choice for skin
   areas
4 oz (208 yds) of 4-ply
   yarn in a color of
   your choice for the
   scale areas
Stitch marker
Yarn needle
Small amounts of black
   and red crochet
   thread for eyes and
   lips
4 oz (208 yds) of
   chunky yarn in the
   colors of your choice
   for the hair
Embellishments

TAIL FINS (MAKE 2)

1 Ch 13.

2 Sc in second Ch from hook.

3 Hdc in next stitch, Dc in next 3 stitches, Trc in next 3 stitches.

4 Dc in next 3 stitches, {Hdc, Ch 2, Sl St in last Ch}.

5 Working in the reverse side, Ch 2, Hdc in first stitch, Dc in next 3 stitches, Trc in next 3 stitches, Dc in next 3 stitches, Hdc in next stitch, Sc in last stitch.

6 Ch 3, Sc in third Ch from hook, Sl St in first Sc made.

7 Ch 1, Rev Sc around the entire fin.

8 Fasten off and weave in the end.

BODY AND HEAD

Hold the wide ends of the fins together at 45-degree angle to form the tail. Leaving a long tail for sewing, connect the two with a Sl St.

Ch 2.

Rd 1 Place 6 Hdc stitches in that one place through both fins to join.

Fold Hdc stitches in half (wrong side together) to start working in rounds. Continue working in rounds moving the stitch marker up as you go. Use the long tail to close any opening there might be at the base of the fins.

Rd 2 1 Hdc in each stitch around (6).

Rd 3 {2 Hdc, 1 Hdc} around (9).

Rd 4 1 Hdc in each stitch around (9).

Rd 5 {2 Hdc, 1 Hdc twice} around (12).

Rd 6 1 Hdc in each stitch around (12).

Rd 7 {2 Hdc, 1 Hdc twice} around (16).

Rd 8 1 Hdc in each stitch around (16).

Rd 9 {2 Hdc, 1 Hdc 3 times} around (20).

Rd 10 {2 Hdc, 1 Hdc 3 times} around (25).

Rd 11 1 Hdc in each stitch around (25).

Rd 12 {2 Hdc, 1 Hdc 4 times} around (30).

Rd 13 {2 Hdc, 1 Hdc 4 times} around (36).

Rd 14 1 Hdc in each stitch around (36).

Rd 15 {2 Hdc, 1 Hdc 5 times} around (42).

Rd 16–17 1 Hdc in each stitch around (42).

Rd 18 {2 Hdc Tog, 1 Hdc in next 2 stitches} 2 Hdc Tog (31).

Rd 19–21 1 Hdc in each stitch around (31).

Stuff and change to skin color.

In order to change color: Yo, insert hook into next stitch, place new color on hook and pull through all 3 loops on hook, continue with new color.

Rd 22 {2 Hdc, 1 Hdc 3 times} 2 Hdc, 1 Hdc in next 2 stitches (39).

Rd 23–24 1 Hdc in each stitch around (39).

Rd 25 {2 Hdc Tog, 1 Hdc twice} 2 Hdc Tog, 1 Hdc (29).

Rd 26 2 Hdc Tog around, 1 Hdc in last stitch (15).

Rd 27 1 Hdc in each stitch around (15).

Good time to do some more stuffing.

Rd 28 2 Hdc in each stitch around (30).

Rd 29–32 1 Hdc in each stitch around (30).

Rd 33 2 Hdc Tog around (15).

Stuff, stuff, stuff.

Rd 34 2 Hdc Tog around, 1 Hdc in last stitch (8).

Sc in next stitch, Sl St in next stitch.

Fasten off, leaving long tail for sewing. Finish stuffing.

Weave through the 8 remaining stitches and draw closed. Make a couple of slip-knots to fully secure, and draw the remaining end down into your work. You may want to anoint the end with the appropriate oil before it is tucked away.

FACE AND HAIR

Decide where the front of your doll is. Do this by fin alignment. I like the fins to be facing the front.

Embroider a simple face. I usually just do closed eyes by making a straight line and drawing it down into a shallow U shape with a few lashes and adding a V shape for the mouth.

Cut chunky hair yarn into 18-inch lengths, fold them in half, and attach each to the head with a lark's head knot. This is the most tedious part, so you can make the hair as thick as you have the patience for. I will not judge you if you just circle the head a few times and give her a high ponytail.

ARMS (MAKE 2)

Ch 2.

Rd 1 6 Hdc in second Ch from hook.

Rd 2 2 Hdc in each stitch around (12).

Rd 3–12 1 Hdc in each stitch around (12).

Sc in next stitch, Sl St in next stitch.

Fasten off, leaving a long tail for sewing.

Sew the open ends to the doll at the shoulders.

Tack the end of one arm to the side of the head and the other to the waist.

BREASTS (MAKE 2)

Ch 2.

Rd 1 6 Sc in second Ch from hook.

Rd 2 2 Sc in each stitch around (12).

Rd 3 {2 Hdc, 1 Hdc} around (18).

Rd 4 1 Hdc in each stitch around (18).

Sc in next stitch, Sl St in next stitch.

Fasten off, leaving a long tail for sewing.

Sew them to the front of the body so that the line between the scale and skin color is just below the halfway point. It should look as if she is wearing a corset.

EMBELLISHMENT

Now it is embellishment time. I have been known to make a headband from beads. Maybe sew ribbon roses or seashells down the sides. She would love a necklace or a belt, don't you think? How about a spiral embroidered on her belly? Treat her like the goddess that she is and dress her regally.

Chapter 9

Advanced Fiber Magick Crochet: Sigils

At the risk of sounding confused, I call some of the shapes I crochet sigils. The reason I call them sigils is because to me they are a focal point containing all the energy of my intention. I create them with focus, much like drawing a sigil on paper, and then charge them according to their particular purpose. Once realized, they can then be put on something as an appliqué or stand on their own on an altar. You can release the energy by burning or burying it, just like a paper sigil. I like to say they are a tangible expression of your intention, so maybe you could call them "tangibles." No matter what you choose to call them, to me they are sigils and quite powerful.

I have seen evidence that sigils can manifest themselves in our lives. If we happen to see the same shape or character appear again and again in random places, we should pay attention to it and think about what it might mean. Of course, sometimes we have no idea what we are supposed to be paying attention to. I have been using the Strega sigil for good fortune under my name for as long as I

Sigils can be enhanced using embroidery stitches. The back stitch is when you work backward, inserting the needle and coming back out halfway from where the stitch started. Come up through the yarn for a cleaner line. Long stitches are when you place one length of yarn from one point to the next. Avoid making them too long or you will risk the project getting snagged on everything.

can remember, never knowing what it was. It served as a nice affirmation when I realized the significance.

These examples convey the idea that a small sigil can hold huge emotional energy. This is the essence of "a picture painting a thousand words." The reason why they work is that they delight our inner child.

Sigils are the decoder ring at the bottom of the cosmic Cracker Jack box. Our younger self will play with it long after we have donned our sensible shoes and gone to work. And that is exactly what we want to have happen. There is no longer any reason to worry about the outcome. It has been taken care of. All we need to do now is watch for the subtle changes that foreshadow our desire taking shape. We can encourage this manifestation by living as if it has already happened, the ensured expectation of things not yet beheld. In other words, faith.

Follow all the steps of basic Fiber Magick as outlined in chapter 1 when creating all the following sigils. Treat their creation as a spell or ritual that culminates in a tangible expression of your magick. So ground and center, cast a circle, raise the energy, set the intention, visualize, and release that energy into the sigil. I have included a third eye meditation (page 191) for the third eye sigil because it is designed to open that sight. This preparation tool could be used anytime. The color wheel meditation (page 46) or the meditation for the as above, so below sigil (page 209) can be used as preparation as well.

Pentagram Sigil

- -

The upward point of the star is representative of spirit. The other four points going clockwise all represent an element: air, fire, water, and earth. Stitch the lines in one smooth rhythm, only stopping at each point for an extra stitch to create a sharp turn and emphasize the direction.

SKILL LEVEL
Beginner

FINISHED SIZE
4"

YOU WILL NEED
1 oz (52 yds) of 4-ply yarn
Crochet hook size H/8 5.00 mm
Stitch marker
5 ball-head straight pins
36" length of contrasting yarn
Yarn needle

INSTRUCTIONS

Ch 2.

Rd 1 6 Sc on second Ch from hook (6).

Rd 2 2 Sc in each stitch around (12).

Rd 3 {1 Sc, 2 Sc} around (18).

Rd 4 {2 Sc, 1 Sc twice} around (24).

Rd 5 Make 1 additional 2 Sc in next St, Sl St in next stitch, Rev Sc in each St around (25).

Fasten off and weave in the ends.

Place straight pins evenly around circle in every fifth stitch to mark the 5 points of the pentagram. Number any pin 1, and then number 2 through 5 clockwise. Thread a large needle with contrasting yarn and use an embroidery stitch such as a backstitch or long stitch to embroider the lines of the pentagram in the following order: 1–3–5–2–4–1. When using the long stitch, weave the last two lines under and over the existing yarn. Either way, tack at each pin to create pointy points.

CHARGING

Present your finished piece to each of the four cardinal directions as you trace the pentacle with your finger.

Heart Sigil

This symbol of love could be worked on while you think about someone in particular or even the world at large. Goddess knows the world could use a little more love. Try this and place it on your altar when the news of the day starts getting you down. It could also make an excellent coaster for your chalice.

Your heartfelt intention might look good in pink or red or even green to align with the heart chakra. It is all up to you. A tangible expression of your heart's desire can be kept as a reminder or given away.

SKILL LEVEL
Beginner

FINISHED SIZE
4"

YOU WILL NEED
1 oz (52 yds) of red,
   pink, or green yarn
Crochet hook size H/8
   5.00 mm

INSTRUCTIONS

Recite the words in italics as you crochet:

1 Ch 3.

Maiden, Mother, Crone.

2 13 Hdc in third chain from hook.

3 Sl St on top of Ch 3.

1, 2, 3, 4, 5, 6, 7, 8, 9, 10, 11, 12, 13 witches in a ring.

4 Ch 3, 2 Dc, picot, 3 Dc in first stitch.

1, 2, 3 to dance, joined by 1, 2, 3 to sing.

5 1 Dc in next 4 stitches.

Earth, fire, water, air.

6 3 Trc in next 2 stitches.

1, 2, 3 will help, 1, 2, 3 will care.

7 Ch 3, Sl St in next stitch, Ch 3.

As below, so above.

8 3 Trc in next 2 stitches.

1, 2, 3 twice over, 1, 2, 3 for my love.

9 1 Dc in next 4 stitches.

Earth, water, air, fire.

10 Sl St on top of beginning Ch 3.

11 Rev Sc around.

Lead me to my heart's desire.

CHARGING

Hold this heart to your heart and recite the following:

Father, Mother, God, and Goddess,
I want to share your many blessings.
Send them where they are most needed,
Always for the greater good.

Goddess Sigil

This sigil will require a color change. When you need to change to the next color when doing a Hdc, the steps are Yo, insert hook in next stitch, Yo, pull through, place the new color yarn over hook, pull through all 3 loops, drop the old color, and continue with the new color.

SKILL LEVEL
Intermediate

FINISHED SIZE
5"

YOU WILL NEED
Crochet hook size H/8
5.00 mm
1 oz (52 yds) each of 2
contrasting yarns

INSTRUCTIONS

1 Ch 2.

2 12 Hdc in second Ch from hook, Sl St in first Hdc made.

3 Ch 1, 2 Hdc in next 2 stitches, changing to new color, 2 Hdc in next 10 stitches in back loops only, changing back to first color, Sl St in first Hdc made (24).

4 Ch 1, {2 Hdc, 1 Hdc} around (36).

5 Ch 1, Hdc 6 times, turn (6).

6 Ch 1, 2 Hdc Tog, 1 Hdc twice, 2 Hdc Tog, turn (4).

7 Ch 1, 2 Hdc Tog twice, turn (2).

8 Ch 1, 2 Hdc Tog, turn.

9 Ch 1, Rev Sc around.

10 Fasten off and weave in the ends.

CHARGING

If you have made this sigil to represent a particular goddess, then call her by name. If not, then call her Mother.

Peace Sign Sigil

You can try different oils on each strand of yarn to direct peace to a particular situation. Combine lavender with rose for a peaceful heart, with pine for a peaceful spirit, or with cinnamon for peace of mind. You can go crazy with this. Remember, the sky is the limit when it comes to Fiber Magick.

SKILL LEVEL
Beginner

FINISHED SIZE
3"

YOU WILL NEED
1 oz (52 yds) each of
    two contrasting
    yarns
2 drops of lavender oil
Crochet hook size H/8
    5.00 mm

INSTRUCTIONS

1 Anoint the ends of each colored yarn with a drop of the lavender oil. Breathe deeply and relax. Allow yourself to find feelings of peace and calm. Transfer these to the yarn as you go.

2 Ch 3 with the yarn you'll use for the center.

3 8 Hdc in third Ch from hook.

4 Sl St into first stitch. As you do, imagine that peace is filling you up.

5 Ch 2.

6 2 Hdc in each stitch around (16).

7 Sl St into first stitch.

8 Fasten off. As you do, imagine that peace is spreading out around you.

9 Join the second yarn: Ch 1, Sc in same stitch.

10 Long Sc in center of the circle. To do this, insert hook into the center of the circle, Yo, draw long loop through center until it reaches the outside of the circle, Yo, and pull through both loops. Do not skip stitch behind long stitch.

11 Sc in next 6 stitches.

12 Long Sc in center of the circle. Do not skip stitch behind long stitch.

13 Sc in next 2 stitches.

14 Long Sc in center of the circle. Do not skip stitch behind long stitch.

15 Sc in next 2 stitches.

16 Long Sc in center of the circle. Do not skip stitch behind long stitch.

17 Sc in next 5 stitches.

18 Sl St in first Sc made.

19 Fasten off.

CHARGING

Hold up your sigil, take a deep breath, and feel the overflow of peace fill you up. Keep all that you need. Let the excess saturate your little peace sign.

Advanced Fiber Magick Crochet: Sigils

Angel Sigil

- -

This little angel could store your energy when you are feeling calm, and then it will remind you of that feeling when you are not so calm. Carry it with you or give it as a gift. You can make it in different colors to convey different messages.

SKILL LEVEL
Intermediate

FINISHED SIZE
4"

YOU WILL NEED
1 oz (52 yds) of 4-ply
 yarn
Crochet hook size H/8
 5.00 mm

INSTRUCTIONS

1 Ch 3.

2 13 Hdc in third Ch from hook.

3 Sl St in top of Ch 3.

4 Ch 3, 3 Dc, Ch 3, Sl St in same stitch.

5 Sl St in next 3 stitches.

6 Ch 2, Hdc, Dc, Hdc, Ch 2, Sl St in same stitch.

7 Sl St in next 3 stitches.

8 Ch 3, 3 Dc, Ch 3, Sl St in same stitch.

9 Sl St in next 3 stitches.

10 Ch 4, 5 Trc, Ch 4, Sl St in same stitch.

11 Sl St in next 3 stitches.

12 Fasten off.

CHARGING

Hold the sigil to your heart center and recite,

Little angel, spread your wings.
Fly where needed. Fix all things.
Spread your love to one and all.
Comfort all who heed your call.

Dragonfly Sigil

- -

Dragonflies like to be around water, so they have become associated with emotions and feelings. Some folks see them as a visit from the spirits of their beloved dead. Others may see them as a sign that change is coming, and that will always evoke some strong emotions indeed. No matter what they signify, they sure are beautiful and fun to watch.

Using four-ply worsted weight yarn and an H hook makes a six-inch motif. Experiment with different yarns and hooks to make a variety of sizes. I've put them on bags and pouches for tarot cards or dice. One would also be at home on a hat right above your third eye.

SKILL LEVEL
Intermediate

FINISHED SIZE
6"

YOU WILL NEED
Crochet hook size H/8
5.00 mm
1 oz (52 yds) of 4-ply yarn

INSTRUCTIONS

1 Ch 18 (body).

2 4 Dc in third Ch from hook, Ch 2, Sl St in same Ch (head).

3 Sc in next 2 Ch on body.

4 Ch 8, Hdc in second Ch from hook, Dc in next 5 Ch, Hdc in next Ch, Sc into side of Sc on body, Sl St into same stitch on body (first wing made).

5 Ch 6, Hdc in second Ch from hook, Dc in next 3 Ch, Hdc in next Ch.

6 Sl St into same Ch on body (second wing made).

7 Sc in next 13 Ch. Do not turn.

8 Sc in opposite side of 13 stitches.

9 Ch 6, Hdc in second Ch from hook, Dc in next 3 Ch, Hdc in next Ch, Sc into side of Sc on body, Sl St into same Ch on body (third wing made).

10 Ch 8, Hdc in second Ch from hook, Dc in next 5 Ch, Hdc in next Ch, Sl St into same Ch on body, Sc in next Ch on body, Sl St into next Ch (fourth wing made).

11 Leave a long tail and fasten off.

12 Use the tail to close up any stretched-out chains due to so many stitches in the same chain if needed.

13 Block and shape.

CHARGING

Hold this talisman to your lips and say,

> Born from water to soar through air,
> Help me speak my truth through all transformations.

Advanced Fiber Magick Crochet: Sigils

Yin-Yang Sigil

Yin and yang are a study in opposites. The symbol is a depiction of how these opposite forces can actually complement each other and support each other. They say opposites attract, and in this case they just cannot get along without each other. Light and darkness, chaos and order, hunger and abundance. It is hard to imagine one without knowing the other. Yin represents female energy, darkness, the moon, and the spirit of all things. Yang represents male energy, light, the sun, and the form of all things. Together they bring balance to the universe.

SKILL LEVEL
Advanced

FINISHED SIZE
6"

YOU WILL NEED
3 drops of rose oil
3 drops of cinnamon oil
1 oz of water
Spray bottle
Crochet hook size H/8
   5.00 mm
1 oz (52 yds) each of 2
   contrasting colors of
   4-ply yarn
Yarn needle

PREPARATION

Prepare a spray with which to charge the finished piece by placing rose oil (yin), cinnamon oil (yang), and water into a spray bottle. Shake well.

CENTERS (MAKE 2)

1 Ch 4 with the first yarn.

2 15 Dc in fourth Ch from hook.

3 Join in top of Ch 4 (16).

4 Fasten off.

5 Make another with the second yarn.

6 Join the second yarn in any Dc on center of first yarn with Sl St.

WORK AROUND THE CIRCLE

Ch 1, Sc in same stitch, 2 Sc in next stitch, Sc in next stitch, 2 Sc in next stitch, Hdc in next stitch, 2 Hdc in next stitch, Hdc in next stitch, 2 Hdc in next stitch, Dc in next stitch, 2 Dc in next stitch, Dc in next stitch, 2 Dc in next stitch, Trc in next stitch, 2 Trc in next stitch, Trc in next stitch, 4 Trc in last stitch in circle.

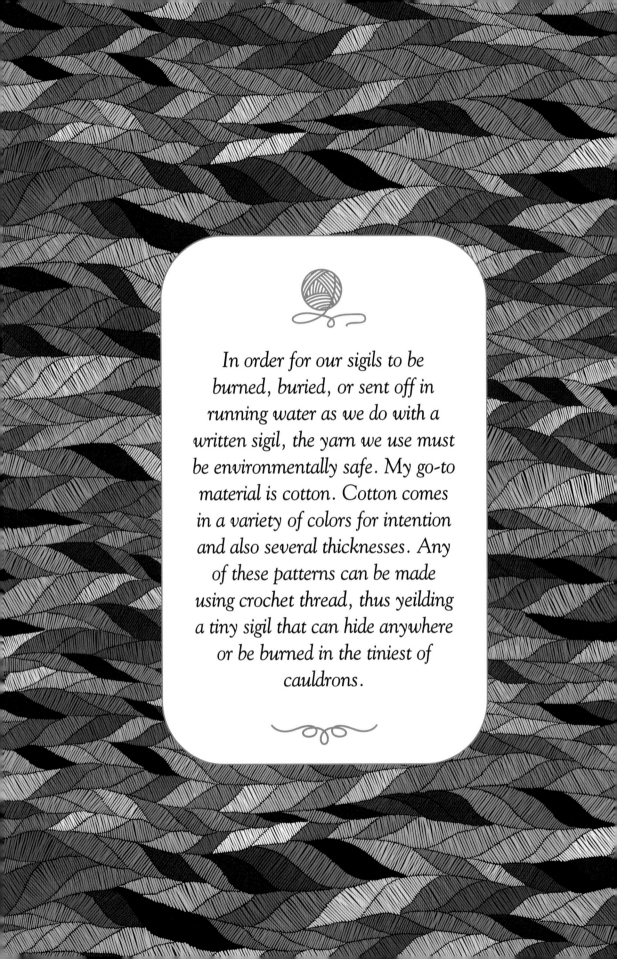

In order for our sigils to be burned, buried, or sent off in running water as we do with a written sigil, the yarn we use must be environmentally safe. My go-to material is cotton. Cotton comes in a variety of colors for intention and also several thicknesses. Any of these patterns can be made using crochet thread, thus yeilding a tiny sigil that can hide anywhere or be burned in the tiniest of cauldrons.

Now start working in rows:

Row 1 Working on the side of last Trc, Ch 4, Trc 3 times, Dc, evenly across the length of the Trc stitch, Dc in next Sc, Hdc in next 2 stitches, Sc in next 2 stitches, Ch 1, and turn.

Row 2 Sc in same stitch, Hdc in next 3 stitches, Dc in next 3 stitches, Trc in next 2 stitches, leave top of Ch 4 unworked, Ch 4, and turn.

Row 3 (Ch 4 counts as first Trc), Trc in next 2 stitches, Dc in next 2 stitches, Hdc in next 2 stitches, Sc in next 2 stitches, Ch 1, and turn.

Row 4 Sc in same stitch, Sc in next stitch, Hdc in next 2 stitches, Dc in next 2 stitches, Trc in next 2 stitches, leave top of Ch 4 unworked, Ch 4, and turn.

Row 5 (Ch 4 counts as first Trc), Trc in next stitch, Dc in next stitch, Hdc in next stitch, Sc next 2 stitches Tog, Sc next 2 Tog, Ch 1, and turn.

Row 6 Sc in same stitch, Hdc in next stitch, Dc in next stitch, Trc in next 2 stitches, leave top of Ch 4 unworked, Ch 4, and turn.

Row 7 (Ch 4 counts as first Trc), Trc in next stitch, Dc in next stitch, Hdc in next stitch, Sc in next stitch, Ch 1, and turn.

Row 8 Sc in same stitch, Hdc in next stitch, Dc in next stitch, Trc in next stitch, leave top of Ch 4 unworked.

Fasten off.

Repeat with second yarn as the center circle and first yarn around.

Flip one piece and fit the pieces together, stretching points to create a circle.

Use the lighter-colored yarn to sew the halves together down the center.

Sc around the outside of one half of the circle evenly using the contrasting color. Change colors halfway through by inserting hook in next stitch and drawing up the new color. Crochet over the old color for a few stitches, then cut off. Continue in the new color to end and Sl St in the first Sc made.

CHARGING
Spray the piece with the oil mixture and block the piece into a circle. Let it dry flat.

Ankh Sigil

- -

The ankh contains strong male and female symbolism. It is used to represent both God and Goddess combined—in other words, the universal power of creation. Many early Egyptian artworks depict this sacred symbol being worn or held by gods and kings. To the Egyptians, the ankh was the ancient symbol of eternal life and resurrection, often referred to as the "key of life." It was a symbol of immortality.

SKILL LEVEL
Intermediate

FINISHED SIZE
5"

YOU WILL NEED
1 oz (52 yds) of 4-ply yarn
Crochet hook size H/8 5.00 mm

INSTRUCTIONS

1 Ch 15.

2 5 Sc, leaving the rest unworked.

3 {Ch 3, Dc in third Ch from hook} 3 times.

4 Sl St in same Ch as last Sc.

5 Ch 6, 5 Sc, Sl St in same Ch again.

6 2 Sc, 7 Hdc completing all unworked Ch.

7 Ch 1, turn, Sc evenly all the way around, skipping a stitch when you get to a concave spot and adding an extra one to go around the corners.

8 Fasten off and weave in the ends.

CHARGING
Place this sigil out in the sun for the high noon hour in order to absorb the power of the sun.

Third Eye Sigil

- -

The third eye resides right in the middle of the forehead. It is the mind's eye that sees more than the material world. Meditation is a good way to open this spiritual eye, so we use this method to prepare ourselves. The meditation included here strives to stimulate each of the five senses. Visualize the scenario by imagining sight, sound, smell, taste, and touch. This will encourage the third eye to open. The sigil created afterward will not be just any eye but one that sees all.

If you are sewing this sigil to an item, you may want to block and flatten it. If you do not block and flatten this piece, it will be rounded just like an eyeball. That is perfect for table decorations or altar elements. You could achieve even more of a 3D effect by sewing it on something and stuffing it ever so lightly before the last few stitches are made.

SKILL LEVEL
Intermediate

FINISHED SIZE
4"

YOU WILL NEED
Crochet hook size H/8
   5.00 mm
6 yds each of yarn in
   black, white, and
   your choice of eye
   color

PREPARATION
Record the meditation on the next page and listen to it before making the project.

MEDITATION
The Third Eye

Take three deep, cleansing breaths and relax. Let your arms lie loosely in your lap and let your head nod forward as if asleep. Melt into the chair and let your breath become steady and slow. We are leaving our physical body behind and going to a party in our minds.

Walk up to the door and knock three times. The door opens and you walk inside. There are wonderous sights to behold. Take in your surroundings, all the colors and rich furnishings. Everything is magnificently appointed. Nothing is out of place. You are surrounded by a rainbow of colors and patterns, each one more fanciful than the next. The room is a masterpiece.

As you drink in the splendor, you start to notice there is music. A group of musicians is playing your favorite tune, and it is being played expertly. You cannot help but move along to the beat of your personal anthem. Everyone is smiling, talking, laughing, and singing a symphony of sight and sound.

Coming to the sitting area, you feel invited to have a seat. The sofa is covered in the most luxurious fabrics. Pillows and throws are available for your comfort. You make yourself at home and sink into the rich textures.

A tray is passed filled with teacups and mugs. Each cup is a work of art in china or pottery. There is one that stands out to you, and you accept it gratefully. You bring it to your lips and breathe in the fragrant aroma. It is your favorite. Allow yourself a moment to enjoy the scent before you drink. When you do drink, you find the beverage to be expertly concocted. It is perfect, not too sweet, not too bitter, just right. Drink and be satisfied.

Bask in this perfection of sight, sound, touch, smell, and taste for as long as you like.

After a while, you begin to notice that the combination of all five of your senses is giving rise to a sixth sense.

Your sight becomes a swirl of light.

You hear the deep chant of *om*.

You feel a tingling up and down your spine.

You smell the sweet perfume of Mother Earth.

You taste pure honey on your tongue.

Your third eye opens, and you are ready to create your masterpiece.

Advanced Fiber Magick Crochet: Sigils

INSTRUCTIONS

Rd 1 Using the black yarn, Ch 3.

12 Dc in third Ch from hook.

Sl St into first Dc made.

Fasten off.

Rd 2 Attach the eye color yarn to any stitch with Sl St.

Ch 1.

2 Hdc in each stitch around (24).

Sl St in first Hdc made.

Fasten off.

Rd 3 Attach the white yarn to any stitch with Sl St.

Ch 1.

Sc in next 5 stitches, Hdc in next stitch, 2 Hdc in next stitch.

Dc in next stitch, 3 Dc in next stitch, Dc in next stitch.

2 Hdc in next stitch, Hdc in next stitch, Sc in next 5 stitches.

Hdc in next stitch, 2 Hdc in next stitch.

Dc in next stitch, 3 dc in next stitch, Dc in next stitch.

2 Hdc in next stitch, Hdc in next stitch.

Sl St in first Hdc made.

Fasten off.

Rd 4 Attach the black yarn to any stitch with Sl St.

Sc in each stitch around.

Rev Sc in each stitch around.

Fasten off and weave in your ends.

CHARGING

Hold this sigil to your third eye and remain present, experiencing all five senses for a while.

Triple Moon Sigil

This sigil can be used to add the power of the Triple Goddess to an item or altar. Made in three parts, it can be sewn together as one. Together they represent the three moon phases: waxing, full, and waning. Arrange them with the full moon in the middle and a crescent on each side. Flip the second crescent so it is facing out from center to represent the waning moon.

Place each one on a separate candle cozy to get a three-candle Triple Goddess set. I have made this sigil in white and put them on black cozies. I have made this sigil in black and placed them on different color cozies, white for the maiden, red for the mother, and gray for the crone.

SKILL LEVEL
Intermediate

FINISHED SIZE
6"

YOU WILL NEED
Crochet hook size H/8
  5.00 mm
1 oz (52 yds) of 4-ply
  yarn

FULL MOON (MAKE 1)

1 Ch 3.

2 15 Dc in third Ch from hook.

3 Sl St in top of Ch 3.

4 Rev Sc in each stitch around (16).

5 Sl St and fasten off, leaving a long tail for sewing.

CRESCENT MOON (MAKE 2)

1 Ch 8.

2 Sc in second Ch from hook.

3 Hdc in next stitch, Dc in next stitch, 3 Dc in next stitch.

4 Dc in next stitch, Hdc in next stitch, Sc and Sl St in next stitch.

5 Do not turn, Ch 1 and Rev Sc back to first stitch.

6 Sl St and fasten off, leaving a long tail for sewing.

7 Pull on the ends of the crescent to shape.

CHARGING

Arrange the three pieces in the triple moon pattern and declare them Maiden, Mother, and Crone.

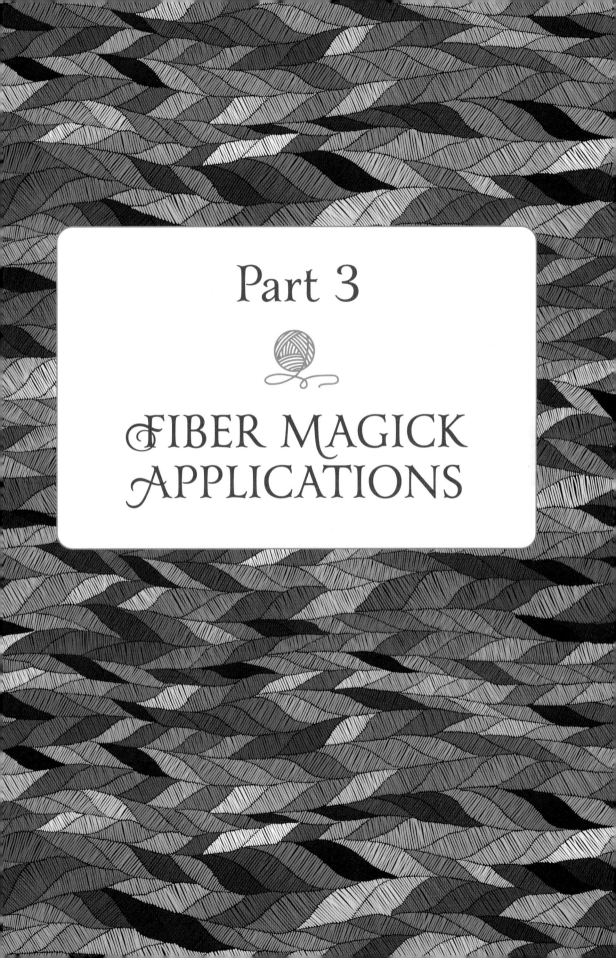

Part 3

FIBER MAGICK
APPLICATIONS

Chapter 10

Healing and Care

Caring for yourself and others is an age-old job of the witch. In this chapter there are projects that can be used to promote healing, both physically and emotionally. Being able to give a gift that keeps on giving through the magick put there is a blessing. May all the kindness you give come back to you by the rule of three.

When we call upon healing energies to support those in need, we are making an effort to treat the whole person. We would never want to discourage someone from following their doctor's orders, but encourage them to add spirit to their regimen. In this way we allow the body to work with the medicine for a much better outcome. Comfort and peace of mind are health boosters. A positive attitude can go a long way in healing as well as acting as a preventative measure. Of course, we cannot share with others what we do not possess.

First, Self-Care

Witch, heal thyself! We can't begin to help others without first showing a little TLC to ourselves. Guarding our energy so that we have some to give is

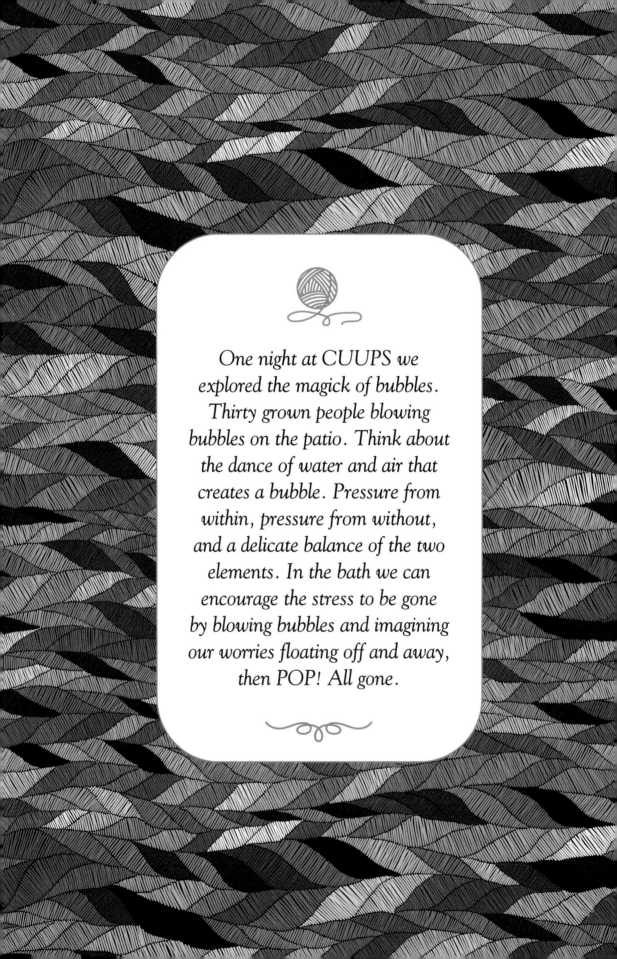

One night at CUUPS we explored the magick of bubbles. Thirty grown people blowing bubbles on the patio. Think about the dance of water and air that creates a bubble. Pressure from within, pressure from without, and a delicate balance of the two elements. In the bath we can encourage the stress to be gone by blowing bubbles and imagining our worries floating off and away, then POP! All gone.

essential. Saying no—or as I like to say, "nomaste"—once in a while may be necessary. "I feel you, but just no." Before you get exhausted, make a habit of carving out some me time. I know you're busy. There's lots to do every day, and I know many of us spend most of our day assisting others, whether personally or professionally. Nevertheless, it's vital to restore, recharge, and repair yourself each day, and sometimes the only way to get some me time is to carve it out of stone! Even fifteen minutes completely to yourself with no other obligations can be enough to recharge. Sit and read a magazine. Have a cup of tea. Take a bubble bath or a hot shower. Go for a walk or sit in nature. Turn off your cell phone and leave the laptop behind. Don't answer the phone and don't respond to requests for your attention. Be vigilant about your me time. Let nothing and no one disturb you. If you've never carved out time for yourself, you'll be amazed at what happens when you start doing it. It's like putting in fresh batteries. You come back restored and replenished and ready to give some more.

Nothing conjures up the image of self-pampering like the luxurious bubble bath. Many of us enjoy a good ritual bath from time to time. Soaking away the mundane world puts us in a better frame of mind for spellwork and ritual, so why not create washcloths imbued with the appropriate Fiber Magick to get the job done?

First, choose the intention needed to perform your chosen task. Be specific about what would bring about a more peaceful environment. Organizational skills? Compassion between family members? Understanding of your needs? Keep that intention through the process of your choice. Whether you choose to crochet, knit, or weave your cloth makes little difference. You may even choose to use a washcloth you already have and embellish it with some embroidery. Pair it with the proper scented soap or, better yet, some of your own homemade bath salts. You will have a fine gift for a friend or a powerful tool for yourself.

The following project is a simple crocheted version of a washcloth.

Power Cloth

While you are working, picture yourself relaxing in the tub without a care in the world. Visualize that what is needed to achieve peace is a reality. When it comes time to make the border, imagine that you are fencing that energy within the confines of the cloth.

SKILL LEVEL
Beginner

FINISHED SIZE
10" × 10"

YOU WILL NEED
Crochet hook size H/8 5.00 mm
2 oz (104 yds) of cotton yarn in the appropriate color

INSTRUCTIONS

Ch 25.

Row 1 Dc in fourth Ch from hook, Dc across, Ch 3 and turn (23).

Row 2–10 (Ch 3 counts as Dc) Dc across, Ch 3 and turn.

Sc evenly around, making 2 stitches in the corners.

When finished, recite,

> *Five by five and ten rows tall,*
> *Bring healing light to one in need.*
> *Let this cloth now find its mark.*
> *Sooth ache and pain for one indeed.*

OTHER SHAPES

Of course, your power cloth does not have to be square. There is meaning and therefore power in the shape of things. Let your sacred geometry creative juices get to flowing. Check out the list of shapes in the appendix at the back of this book for some suggestions on shaping your cloth. How would it change the energy if you were to crochet a nice circle?

Bath Salt Bag

- -

While making the bag, focus in the same way you focused on intent while making the power cloth. The bag that holds the salts can take it a step further. Imagine the properties of the salts passing through the bag and absorbing the energies infused there.

SKILL LEVEL
Beginner

FINISHED SIZE
6" × 9"

YOU WILL NEED
2 oz (104 yds) of cotton yarn
Crochet hook size H/8 5.00 mm

INSTRUCTIONS

Ch 16.

Rd 1 1 Sc in second Ch from hook and in next 13 Ch, 2 Sc in next Ch. Do not turn. Working the back side of the foundation Ch, Sc 14, 2 Sc in next Ch. Join with Sl St to first Sc (32).

Rd 2 Ch 3 (counts as first Dc), Dc in next 14 stitches, 2 Dc in next, Dc in next 15 stitches, 2 Dc in next, join (34).

Rd 3 Ch 4 (counts as Dc and Ch 1), skip next stitch, {Dc, Ch 1, skip next stitch} around. Join to third Ch of beginning Ch 4 (17 Dc).

Rd 4–11 Sl St to Ch 1 space, Ch 4, {Dc in next Ch 1 space, Ch 1} around, join with Sl St to third Ch of beginning Ch 4 (17 Dc).

Rd 12 Ch 3 (counts as first Dc), Dc in Ch 1 Sp, {Dc in next stitch, Dc in Ch 1 space} around, join with Sl St to top of Ch 3 (34 Dc).

Rd 13 Ch 1, Rev Sc in each stitch around, join.

Finish off and weave in the ends.

FOR THE TIE

Ch 100. Finish off and weave in the ends.

Weave the tie through round 11.

⟶ SPELL ⟶
Bath Salts Spell to Love Yourself First

Making your own bath salts can add to the intention. This recipe incorporates all four elements and is full of the correspondences of love. It yields four cups.

YOU WILL NEED
2 cups of Epsom salts
Vanilla oil
¼ cup of orange peels, thinly sliced
¼ cup of cinnamon bark chips
¼ cup of rosemary, stems removed
¼ cup of pink Himalayan salt
2 6 × 9-inch organza bags

INSTRUCTIONS
In a large bowl place Epsom salts, add several drops of the vanilla oil, and stir while saying,

Salt of the earth with vanilla sweet
Scrubs away all misery,
Leaves me ready to receive.
All good things will come to me.

Add the orange peel and say,

Orange peel for happiness.
Lifts the spirits, have no doubt.
Sadness doesn't stand a chance.
Breathe love in and worry out.

Add cinnamon bark and say,

Add cinnamon to the mix
Whenever you need a little fire
To burn away a gloomy mood
That keeps you from your heart's desire.

Add the rosemary and say,

Rosemary to heal body and soul,
Languish in the water warm.
Fragrant herb will add delight
And keep away all that harm.

Add the pink salt and say,

Pink salt from the earth,
A mineral of life,
Cleanses away
Undue worry and strife.

Divide the mixture into the organza bags and tie tightly. Now you have one to keep and one to give away. See, pampering yourself has already turned out well for someone else. When you fill the bath, just throw the bag in like a tea bag. The organza will keep the herbs from going down the drain, which makes it much easier to clean the tub afterward. Make it easy on yourself. You deserve it. These bath ritual tea bags can be made for all sorts of purposes. Keep the Epsom salts and pink Himalayan salt and substitute the essential oils and herbs to your liking. There is a list of herbs in the appendix at the back of this book to help.

Connecting to Nature

There is a very wise saying that goes, "You cannot pour from an empty cup." If we desire to fill our handiwork with positive energy, we must be a conduit of that energy, constantly replenishing ourselves as we go along. I like to imagine the Goddess above me pouring silvery, sparkling water down on the top of my head from a silver pitcher by a beautiful well, much like the images you see in paintings and frescoes of Roman or Greek goddesses. It feels so nourishing and refreshing. In this way, I am filled with the sparkling waters of life first, and then the overflow goes into my handiwork. Instead of becoming drained by my practice, I am actually sustained by my practice. I feel more energized for having done it. In addition to this type of visualization, I make a habit of meditation. It does not have to be for very long, but sometime during the day, I like to take a few minutes to myself when I can breathe deeply. During times like this, I let my imagination take me to a happy place.

As Above, So Below Sigil

When I imagine the phrase "as above, so below," I picture a calming effect showering down on the workaday world. I might sometimes see a beam of light and love coming up from the ground because I also see the reverse as true: as below, so above. Trees got it going on in both directions. They pull life-giving energy from the earth and transform it into nourishing fruit. They absorb the sunlight and rain to push their roots even deeper into the ground. They also take our carbon dioxide and make us fresh oxygen. Trees rule! I needed to translate this divine action into a piece of Fiber Magick, so I created this sigil.

SKILL LEVEL
Intermediate

FINISHED SIZE
6"

YOU WILL NEED
Meditation recording
Crochet hook size H/8
 5.00 mm
1 oz (52 yds) of 4-ply
 yarn in the color of
 your intention

PREPARATION
Record the following meditation and play it as you create the sigil. Imagine the divine spirit that surrounds you and be well.

MEDITATION
What Can a Tree Teach Me?

Breathe. Relax. Clear your mind of all the mundane stuff that happens to us humans. Feel your feet on the floor.

Now, down through the floor, your feet become roots. Reach down to the treasures of the earth. Dig down for such treasures as the nourishment from the minerals. Search for the blessings from the waters, the elixir of life. Soak up the energy from our Blessed Mother, Gaia.

Feel the energy from the stones and bones. Become aware of the wisdom of the ancestors, the knowledge of past lives, the ones who came before us. They knew what it was like to live as part of the Mother. Before our modern internet, there was this network of absolute truth. Pull as much of this beautiful energy as you need. The Mother has no limits. Take this energy up through the roots you have sent into the earth.

Now, you can grow, reaching for the sky. Allow your body to become the trunk and your arms the branches. Reach for the stars. Become a home for birds and bees. Become the shade for the family picnic. Become the provider of nourishing fruit. Become the connection to the Mother's love. Enjoy the breeze as you stretch yourself up over the ground below.

As above, so below. Send your roots even deeper, digging down into the vast knowledge that our Mother offers. Seek out the nourishment that is waiting for you. Thirst after this knowledge. Welcome it from all sources. Process it. Use it, and then send it on.

You are an important cog in the Great Machine. You are a tree. You will live on forever in the Cosmic Web. So mote it be.

Breathe deeply. In and out. Come back to your human self. Come back to this room, but do not sever those roots. Humans need roots too.

INSTRUCTIONS

1 Ch 13.

2 1 Hdc in second Ch from hook, 1 Hdc in each stitch across (12). Do not turn.

3 {Ch 7, *Sl St in second Ch from hook, Sl St in next 2 Ch.*

4 Ch 4 repeat between * *, Ch 4 repeat between * *, Sl St in the same stitch as step 3, Sl St in next 3 Ch}.

5 Sl St in side of last Hdc, repeat between { }.

6 Sl St corner Ch, repeat between { }.

7 Working down the reverse side, Sl St to far corner.

8 Repeat "as above, so below" at the opposite end of your work.

9 Sl St in first Hdc made.

10 Fasten off and weave in the end.

11 Hold the sigil to your heart center and recite,

> Ebb and flow, around we go.
> Branches high and roots down low.
> Stretching, reaching, there's more to know.
> As above, we create below.

Carry it with you to feel grounded.

Caring for Others: Plarning

Plarning is the art of making yarn from plastic grocery bags. All ages can take part. A wide range of crafting skills are needed and can work together. The bags must be flattened and then cut into strips crosswise. This creates rings that are looped together to form lengths of plastic yarn, "plarn."

The beauty of this project is that the act of plarning transforms trash into a benefit for our homeless population. The plarn can be crocheted into mats that offer a moisture barrier for those folks who sleep on the ground. This is a much-appreciated item, especially here in South Florida, where it is always damp if not raining. This layer between blanket and ground cuts down on the bacterial growth in a blanket, which may never otherwise have a chance to fully dry out.

This project not only impacts the person in need who receives the mat, but it also keeps five to seven hundred plastic bags out of the landfill. It will also make a difference to the person working in the recycling plant who does not have to climb down into the mechanism and untangle those bags from the works. The plarn mat project allows people working on the project to feel that they are making a difference, no matter how small.

Plarn (Plastic Yarn)

This project recycles plastic grocery bags that the supermarket supplies. Some craft stores use bags of a similar weight as well. Thick bags that you might get at a clothing store and thin bags that the newspaper or veggies come in are not suitable. Those bags should be recycled in the appropriate bin.

SKILL LEVEL
Beginner

FINISHED SIZE
Varies

YOU WILL NEED
Plastic grocery bags
Scissors

INSTRUCTIONS

1 Flatten and fold the bag lengthwise.

2 Cut off the bottom and handles.

3 Cut the remaining piece into fourths. You will have 4 loops.

4 Connect the loops with a lark's head knot.

5 Repeat and wind the plarn into balls.

Plarn Mat

- -

It takes between five and seven hundred bags to make a mat.

SKILL LEVEL
Beginner

FINISHED SIZE
4' × 6'

YOU WILL NEED
800–1,000 yds of
    plarn
Crochet hook size
    Q/16.00 mm

INSTRUCTIONS

1 Ch 43.

2 Hdc in second Ch from hook, Hdc in each Ch across, Ch 1, turn.

3 Hdc in each stitch across, Ch 1, turn.

4 Repeat until the mat is 6 feet long.

5 Sc evenly down the long side of the mat.

6 Place 2 Sc in the corner.

7 Across the short side 4 Sc, Ch 40 and Sc back, 4 Sc, Ch 40 and Sc back.

8 4 Sc, Sc in next Ch, attaching end of second Ch 40, 4 Sc, Ch 40 and Sc back.

9 4 Sc.

10 Place 2 Sc in the corner.

11 Sc evenly down the long side.

12 Place 2 Sc in the corner.

13 Sc across the short side.

14 Place 2 Sc in the corner.

15 Sl St into first Sc made, fasten off, and weave in the end.

16 Fold the mat lengthwise and roll it up from the plain short end.

17 Tie on each end and handle in the middle.

⟦Bullet⟧ ⟨BLESSING⟩ ⟦Bullet⟧
Blessing the Effort

Before I put a plarn mat in the donation area at the church, after which it will be taken to the shelter and passed out to someone in need, I like to say:

> *Trash to treasure, be of good use.*
> *Provide some small comfort*
> *To those who have need.*
> *So mote it be.*

Even in the plarning circle we have fun with color. We get so excited when there are colored bags in the donation bin. Some of us are purist and want to separate the colors. Others like myself take a more random approach. The trouble with random is of course it is so, well, random. You might get three blue bags in a row and then a white, then a gray, or whatever. It is better to have some planning to your spontaneity. I created a lovely earth and sky plarn ball once by seeking out the blue and brown bags and arranging them in a pleasant "random" order. I'm sure it was appreciated. Aesthetics are important to quality of life no matter what your situation or circumstance. And of course we know that color healing is an accepted practice for many healers.

Healing with Texture

Texture may not be as common when you think of a healing practice, but you have to admit the feel of a cashmere sweater or plush teddy bear can change your mood and lift your spirits. You can use texture for healing and comfort by making a fiddle cuff. You may have seen one. They are wide arm bands with buttons and bobbles attached for folks with dementia to occupy their hands and not scratch or pinch themselves. They are very nice charitable donations that will use up all that leftover novelty yarn or fabric you have stashed away. Just make small square swatches. You can crochet or knit some squares or cut them from cloth. Sew them together to form a cuff. As you do, you can imagine the pieces of cuff representing the pieces of a life being sewn back together. Add the embellishments and you're done. While you're working, set your intention. Try for a calming, peaceful vibe for this one. Intensify the feeling with the textures you choose both in yarn feel and stitch feel.

Fiddle Cuff

What textures would you include in your fiddle cuff? What embellishments would you add? I bet you won't be able to make two alike. This would make a great group project for donating to a nursing home.

There is a list of textures and their correspondences in the appendix at the back of this book.

SKILL LEVEL
Beginner

FINISHED SIZE
12"

YOU WILL NEED
Novelty yarns
Scraps of various
    fabrics
Needle and thread or
    sewing machine
Embellishments
    such as buttons,
    beads, ribbons, or
    embroidery thread

INSTRUCTIONS

1 Create your swatches from all the various scraps you have collected.

2 Arrange them in a 12" × 12" square and sew them together.

3 Sew two sides together to form a tube.

4 Embellish your cuff all over with buttons and ribbons that can be fiddled with.

Texture Mandala

The skill level on this project is advanced because working with a variety of textures is always challenging. Use the pattern for the crocheted mandala outlined on page 134, but in addition to changing colors, change textures as you go. This creates a hands-on meditation tool that can be used by persons who respond to more tactile activities or who are unable to see color.

SKILL LEVEL
Advanced

FINISHED SIZE
24"

YOU WILL NEED
16 oz (832 yds) of
    yarn in a variety of
    textures
24" hula-hoop
Crochet hook size H/8
    5.00 mm

INSTRUCTIONS
Follow the same pattern as for the crocheted mandala on page 134, changing the textures as you go instead of or in addition to changing colors.

Emotional Support Poppets

My crocheted goddess poppets started out short. They were always only six to eight inches tall. I imagined them being used to represent the Goddess on people's altars. They continue to be popular. I get calls for the stylized goddess shape with arms over her head. The Venus of Willendorf style is also quite in demand. These small dolls are perfect for spellwork.

It was not long, however, before the dolls had grown (literally) to include other uses. I've been making them more like sixteen to eighteen inches tall. I've seen them used as throw pillows and decorative pieces. But, of course, my favorite use is as the emotional support poppet. When I crochet one, I keep this in mind and load it with many hugs before it us sent off to its new home. Sometimes it's hard to see them go. I prop them up where I can see them throughout the day. I wait till the last minute to place them in their gift bag or packing box and take them out to the car to begin their journey. Ah, such is life. My children must leave the nest.

Emotional Support Poppet

- -

This poppet pattern can be used to make a variety of emotional support poppets to fit the needs or personality of the recipient. Colors and embellishments can take the doll from spring maiden to goth goddess.

This poppet starts and ends with the power of eight for success and increases by four every other round for stability. The pattern is written in Hdc stitches for a touch of fire. This would be perfect for someone going through a hardship that requires courage and strength. The same pattern could be done in Sc, which represents water for healing. This would be appropriate for illness or grief. It would also result in a smaller poppet. If you would like to do it in Dc for air, I would go down in hook size so that the stitches do not get too loose and let the stuffing show. A size F/5 3.50 mm hook would be a better choice. In any case, infuse it with hugs, and it will be a support for someone who needs it.

SKILL LEVEL
Intermediate

FINISHED SIZE
16"

YOU WILL NEED
7 oz (364 yds) of 4-ply
   yarn in desired color
Crochet hook size H/8
   5.00 mm
Stitch marker
Yarn needle
Embellishments

INSTRUCTIONS

Ch 2.

Rd 1 8 Hdc in second Ch from hook (8).

Rd 2 1 Hdc in each stitch around (8).

Rd 3 {1 Hdc, 2 Hdc} around (12).

Rd 4 1 Hdc in each stitch around (12).

Rd 5 {1 Hdc twice, 2 Hdc} around (16).

Rd 6 1 Hdc in each stitch around (16).

Rd 7 {1 Hdc 3 times, 2 Hdc} around (20).

Rd 8 1 Hdc in each stitch around (20).

Rd 9 {1 Hdc 4 times, 2 Hdc} around (24).

Rd 10 1 Hdc in each stitch around (24).

Rd 11 {1 Hdc 5 times, 2 Hdc} around (28).

Rd 12 1 Hdc in each stitch around (28).

Rd 13 {1 Hdc 6 times, 2 Hdc} around (32).

Rd 14 1 Hdc in each stitch around (32).

Rd 15 {1 Hdc 7 times, 2 Hdc} around (36).

Rd 16 1 Hdc in each stitch around (36).

Rd 17 {1 Hdc 8 times, 2 Hdc} around (40).

Rd 18–20 1 Hdc in each stitch around (40).

At this point you may want to make a spiral of surface stitches on her belly before decreasing and stuffing (see stitch guide in starting on page 105).

Rd 21 {1 Hdc 3 times, 2 Hdc Tog} around (32).

Rd 22 {1 Hdc twice, 2 Hdc Tog} around (24).

Rd 23 1 Hdc in each stitch around (24).

Stuff.

Rd 24 {1 Hdc, 2 Hdc} around (36).

Rd 25–28 1 Hdc in each stitch around (36).

Rd 29 {1 Hdc, 2 Hdc tog} around (24).

Stuff.

Rd 30 2 Hdc Tog around (12).

Rd 31 1 Hdc in each stitch around (12).

Rd 32 2 Hdc in each stitch around (24).

Rd 33–34 1 Hdc in each stitch around (24).

Rd 35 {1 Hdc, 2 Hdc Tog} around (16).

Stuff.

Rd 36 2 Hdc Tog around (8).

Finish stuffing.

Sc in next stitch. Sl St in next stitch. Fasten off, leaving a tail to weave through the remaining 8 stitches. Close and draw the end into the doll.

ARMS

Stuff lightly as you go. The arms will wrap around the top of the head, so you do not want them to be too stiff.

Ch 8, Sl St in first Ch to form a ring.

Rd 1 1 Hdc in each stitch around (8).

Rd 2 2 Hdc in each stitch around (16).

Rd 3–24 1 Hdc in each stitch around (16).

Rd 25 2 Hdc Tog around (8).

Sc in next stitch, Sl St in next stitch. Fasten off, leaving a long tail for sewing.

Stitch the ends of the arms closed, and sew the ends of the arms to the body on either side of the head below the neck.

Embellish as desired. In addition to a spiral on her belly, you could add breasts, hair, and a face as you did with the mermaid.

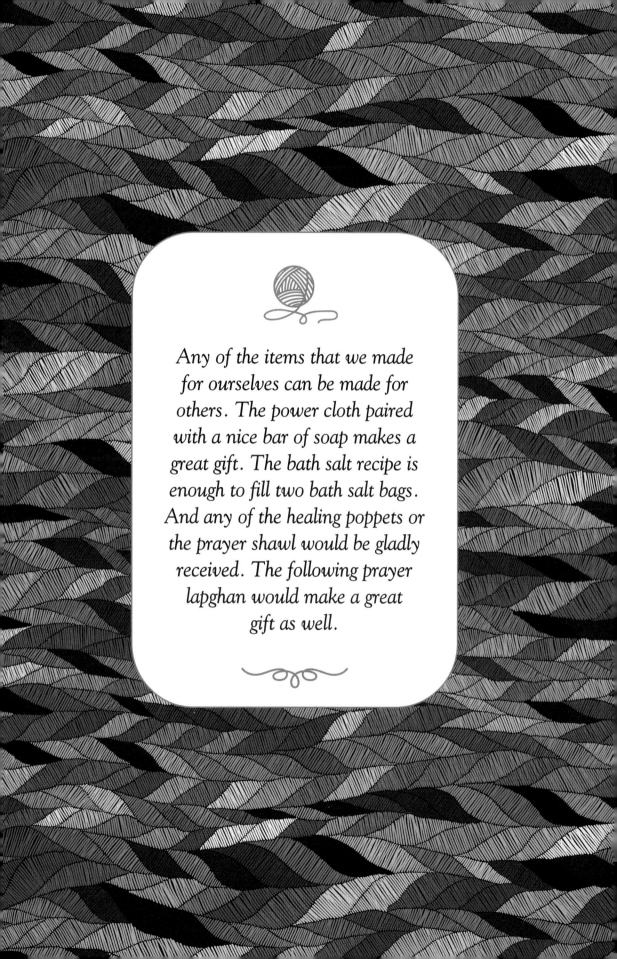

Any of the items that we made for ourselves can be made for others. The power cloth paired with a nice bar of soap makes a great gift. The bath salt recipe is enough to fill two bath salt bags. And any of the healing poppets or the prayer shawl would be gladly received. The following prayer lapghan would make a great gift as well.

Prayer Lapghan

A lapghan is a small blanket. It is just the right size to put over the lap when sitting up in a chair. The meditative quality of this repetitive pattern allows you to fill the blanket with good vibes and blessings of good health. It will be perfect to throw over tired legs and aching knees in the evening.

I took inspiration from the prayer shawl when writing a pattern for a prayer lapghan. The mesh pattern can be made in any size as long as you start with an even number of chains in the foundation. Filling in every other mesh with a Dc makes for a more substantial blanket and gives an introduction to filet crochet. Filet crochet is a technique in which pictures and patterns are made by filling in the mesh squares. The pattern in this blanket is checkerboard.

SKILL LEVEL
Intermediate

FINISHED SIZE
36" × 36"

YOU WILL NEED
28 oz (1,456 yds) of
  4-ply yarn
Crochet hook size J/10
  6.00 mm

INSTRUCTIONS

Ch 100.

Row 1 Dc in sixth Ch from hook, Dc in next 2 stitches, Ch 1, skip next Ch, {Dc in next 3 Ch, Ch 1, skip next Ch, Dc in next 3 Ch} across. Ch 4 and turn.

Row 2 (Ch 4 counts as Dc, Ch 1) skip next stitch, Dc in next 3 stitches, {Ch 1, skip next stitch, Dc in next 3 stitches} across. Ch 4 and turn.

Row 3–50 Repeat row 2.

BORDER

Work around the blanket:

Row 51 Dc in each stitch across, Ch 2, rotate work 90 degrees.

Row 52 2 Dc in side of last stitch on row 51, {2 Dc in Ch Sp, 2 Dc in side of next stitch} across. Ch 2, rotate work 90 degrees.

Row 53–54 Repeat rows 51–52.

SI St into first stitch on row 51.

Rev Sc around to hold in all those good vibes.

Perform the project blessing ritual on page 17.

Healing and Care

Chapter 11

∽

Protection

An ounce of prevention is worth a pound of cure, so the saying goes, and it is certainly true. It is good advice not only in the case of physical disease but also in the case of spiritual dis-ease. Aligning ourselves with love and light acts to refract any negative energies that are going on around us. Like attracts like, so a positive attitude with focus on what is going well in our lives will let the universe know exactly what joys to increase.

The bubble of light we surround ourselves with while in a magickal circle, such as the ones cast in ritual, protects us from outside influences. Visualizing a mirror reflecting ill intent back to its origin is a common practice. Banishing and protection rituals clear out the spiritual and psychic rubbish and make your magick powers more intense. There are symbols, amulets, fetishes, and dolls all intended for the purpose of protecting ourselves, others, and property. We can craft them.

While making items of protection, keep the purpose of the finished item clearly in mind. Start with preparation as the first step of each craft. Meditate on the need of the item. Make yourself comfortable, relaxed, grounded, and determined to

While making items of protection, keep the purpose of the finished item clearly in mind. Start with preparation as the first step of each craft. Meditate on the need of the item. Make yourself comfortable, relaxed, grounded, and determined to accomplish your goal. It is very important to have the right energies filling your work. Take the time to prepare as needed.

accomplish your goal. It is very important to have the right energies filling your work. Take the time to prepare as needed.

Amulets

An amulet is a small object thought to protect the individual from evil. Passing as a piece of jewelry or a decorative object, an amulet can hold powerful protective spells. Gems, coins, or bones can be included in an amulet, the correspondences of which will be carefully chosen to call upon the spirit required to protect and defend the wearer. When we make our own amulets, we are free to imbue them with the protection, luck, or magickal qualities we wish.

Wards

A ward is a spell that acts as a protective barrier around an area or piece of property. It may be temporary, as in the protection you put up around a ritual space, or more permanent, as in the protection you would want around your home. The permanent type needs to be recharged from time to time to stay powerful and effective. A ward guards or watches over a target, and it can also turn something aside. When we drink orange juice to "ward off" a cold, we are calling upon vitamin C and its protective properties. If you don't want anyone to touch your stuff, you might visualize intense heat coming from the items. If we ward the doors of our homes and cars, only those invited may enter.

Protecting Our Loved Ones

When loved ones need to be away from us due to work or play, we worry. When a child or spouse in the military is deployed to a foreign country, we really worry. No matter how far away or how long the stay, it is relieving to know that we have sent protection with them. Worry never solved anything. Worry is a waste of imagination that creates problems that have not happened. Instead, try focusing your energy on a good outcome and sealing it in a tangible object that reminds us that the Goddess is with us. Make an amulet and gift it to someone, and then make a ward frame and put their picture in it to keep them safely in your heart.

Banishing with a Sigil

Creating a sigil while focusing on a threat or danger will help stop it in its tracks. The herbal mixture of garlic and rue will repel anything evil. Using Hdc burns with fire and Sl St at the end of each round gives a definite place to voice your will.

Amulet of Protection

- -

This amulet is a great project to do with children. It features a pocket to slip herbs or sigils inside. The woven pattern can be accentuated by using two different colors. A third color can be used as a border.

SKILL LEVEL
Beginner

FINISHED SIZE
2"

YOU WILL NEED
2 squares of plastic
    canvas, each 2" × 2"
1 oz (52 yds) of cord or
    yarn
Yarn needle
Craft glue
1 flat-backed stone or
    crystal (cabochon)
Cord for hanging
Beads to embellish
    hanging cord

INSTRUCTIONS

1 Create warp on each plastic canvas square by threading the yarn from one side to the other across.

2 Make the weft by rotating the square 90 degrees and weaving over and under the warp before inserting the needle on the other side of the square.

3 Using a whip stitch, sew a border around both squares.

4 Holding the squares together back to back, sew 3 sides together.

5 Glue the stone to one side.

6 Place the beads on the hanging cord.

7 Attach the hanging cord to either end of the open side.

8 Slip the desired herbs or sigils into the pouch.

9 Wear as a necklace or hang on an altar.

Door Ward

A door ward can be nailed to the doorframe or placed above the door out of sight. Add a magnet to the back and place it under your car. This door ward project has two steps. First, you will perform a basic warding spell. Then, you will create the door wards with the remnants of what you gather in the spell.

SKILL LEVEL
Beginner

FINISHED SIZE
3"

YOU WILL NEED
Salt
Water
Small bowl
Fireproof plate
Incense cone
Tea light
½-oz vial with cork or
  lid
2 1" squares of plastic
  canvas
4 1" × 3" rectangles of
  plastic canvas
2 oz (104 yds) of yarn
  in desired colors
Yarn needle
2" magnetic strip and
  glue (optional)

STEP 1: BASIC WARDING SPELL

This warding spell can be done by walking around your property, walking around inside your home, or walking around your car to protect it from thieves and vandals. The physical results of this ritual will be used in step 2.

1 Place the salt and water in the bowl and set it on the plate.

2 Place the cone and tea light on the plate and light both.

3 Carry the plate around the perimeter of the area you wish to ward while reciting,

> *By earth and fire and water and air,*
> *No one causing harm will dare*
> *To enter here by day or night*
> *Or tread the line caused by this rite.*

4 In a vial with a cork or lid, save a bit of the elements from the warding ritual. All you need is a drop of the salt water, a pinch of ash from the incense, and a drip from the candle.

STEP 2: THE DOOR WARD

Now it is time to create your ward. Note that brown and black are usually considered colors of protection. You could fill in the canvas with one color yarn and whip stitch it together with the other. Or you could look for a variegated yarn that includes those two colors and cover the whole thing.

1 Cover the rectangles and squares with stitches.

2 Whip stitch the long sides of the rectangles to each other to form a box open at both ends.

3 Whip stitch a square to one end.

4 Place the vial in the box and whip stitch the other square on top to close it.

5 Make a yarn loop on one of the top corners for hanging.

6 If using under a car, glue a magnetic strip to one of the long sides.

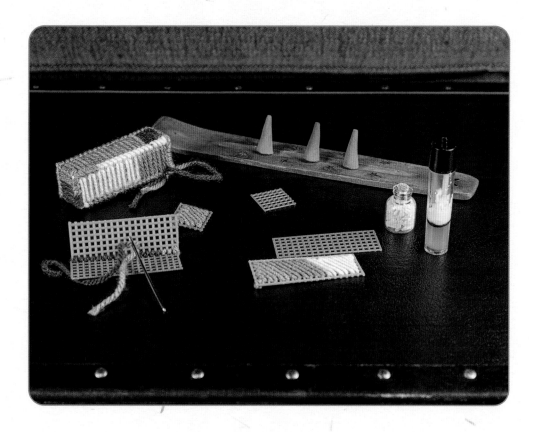

Protection

Besom Cover

- -

Besom is a term used to designate a broom that is used for magickal purposes and is traditionally made of birch twigs bound by willow lashings to an ash or oak branch. Even if we do not have a fancy traditional besom, we can get the same results by dressing up a straw broom. Making a cover for your besom will add the properties of the materials you use.

Placing a besom by the door will act as a ward and protect you and your home from evil spirits. Make sure to place the bristles up and let the shaft hit the floor for optimum protection.

In addition to protecting your property, use this besom to cleanse your ritual space before performing magick. It has the ability to cleanse not just a physical space but also a mental and metaphysical space. When we physically sweep an area, we are also mentally sweeping the area. Once the space is clean and cleansed, the besom stands guard at the door to ensure the dirt stays gone.

Besom covers can also be made to coincide with the season or sabbat.

SKILL LEVEL
Beginner

FINISHED SIZE
9" wide

YOU WILL NEED
New straw broom
9"-wide piece of
    hemmed fabric long
    enough to wrap
    around the broom
Sprigs of eucalyptus
Sprigs of rosemary
Hot glue and gun
Silk flowers, ribbons,
    and beads for
    embellishment
Needle and thread
9" strip of hook and
    loop tape

INSTRUCTIONS

1 Mark the center of the fabric by folding it in half.

2 Lay the fabric strip on a flat surface.

3 Alternate sprigs of eucalyptus (moon, water, earth) and rosemary (sun, fire, air) starting at the center of fabric and extending toward both sides within the width of the broom. Glue them in place.

4 Fill the spaces between the sprigs by sewing or gluing embellishments in a pleasing arrangement.

5 Glue the hook and loop tape to the short ends of the fabric.

6 Wrap the cover around the broom and secure.

Ward Frame

- -

Plastic canvas comes in a wide variety of colors. This frame would look good in black or brown, colors of protection. If you use white, back it with a dark piece of felt. This frame made in a smaller size would make a good luggage tag to protect your suitcase.

SKILL LEVEL
Beginner

FINISHED SIZE
5"

YOU WILL NEED
15 yds each of black, white, gray, and brown yarn
5" × 5" square of plastic canvas
Yarn needle
Felt in dark color or color to match canvas
Sewing needle and thread
Picture of your loved one

INSTRUCTIONS

1 Starting with a different color of yarn in each corner, make 24 long diagonal stitches across the squares.

2 When colors overlap, weave the working yarn through the existing stitches before inserting yarn in the opposite side.

3 The last color will be woven through existing stitches on both ends.

4 Using the color that matches the felt, whip stitch around the entire square to create a finished edge, trying to catch any ends as you go.

5 Tuck in the remaining ends.

6 Sew the felt to the back of the plastic canvas.

7 Carefully tuck the picture of your loved one inside the protection created by the crossed yarns and recite,

> Brown, gray, white, and black,
> Protect my heart till it comes back.
> So mote it be.

"No" Sigil

This sigil can be pinned to a picture of the threat. Please consider the ethics discussed in chapter 8 when directing magick toward a person.

SKILL LEVEL
Beginner

FINISHED SIZE
3"

YOU WILL NEED
6 yds each of 2 contrasting color yarns

Crochet hook size H/8 5.00 mm

¼ tsp garlic powder and minced rue

INSTRUCTIONS

Ch 3.

Rd 1 9 Hdc in third Ch from hook, Sl St in first Hdc and say, "No."

Rd 2 2 Hdc in each stitch around. Sl St in first Hdc and say, "No."

Fasten off and rub the sigil with herbal mixture.

Attach the contrasting color yarn to any Hdc.

Rd 3 {Sc, 2 Sc} around. Sl St in first Sc and say, "No."

Ch 1, bring the yarn to the back of your work and make surface chains across the circle, Sl St in Sc on opposite side.

CHARGING

Ch 1, Rev Sc around to seal the spell and declare, "No."

Warrior Bear

- -

Teddy bears have been protecting small children from the monster under the bed for decades. This little guy has a helmet, sword, and shield to do battle with the ghoulies. Add even more protective magick with herbs, oils, and sigils in the stuffing.

SKILL LEVEL
Intermediate

FINISHED SIZE
9"

YOU WILL NEED
Sigil
1 tsp of chamomile
1 tsp of crushed
    caraway seeds
Stuffing
Stitch marker
Crochet hooks size H/8
    5.00 mm and F/5
    3.75 mm
6 oz (312 yds) of 4-ply
    brown yarn
Black yarn for features
1 oz (52 yds) each of
    white and gray yarn
    for sword and shield
Yarn needle

PREPARATION

1 Create a sigil.

2 Mix the herbs.

3 Flatten out a handful of stuffing and sprinkle with herbs.

4 Draw the sigil in the herbs with finger.

5 Roll up the stuffing so the herbs remain safe inside. Use it in the center of the bear's body.

HEAD AND BODY
Working in rounds, move the stitch marker up at the end of each round.

Using H hook and brown yarn, Ch 2.

Rd 1 6 Hdc in second Ch from hook (6).

Rd 2 2 Hdc in each stitch around (12).

Rd 3 {2 Hdc, 1 Hdc} around (18).

Rd 4 {2 Hdc, 1 Hdc twice} around (24).

Rd 5–7 1 Hdc in each stitch around (24).

Rd 8 {2 Hdc Tog, 1 Hdc twice} around (18).

Rd 9 {1 Hdc, 2 Hdc Tog} around (12).

Rd 10 1 Hdc in each stitch around (12).

Rd 11 2 Hdc in each stitch around (24).

Rd 12 1 Hdc in each stitch around (24).

Stuff the head.

Rd 13 {2 Hdc, 1 Hdc twice} around (32).

Rd 14–19 1 Hdc in each stitch around (32).

Add the magickal stuffing in the center of the body.

Rd 20 {2 Hdc Tog, 1 Hdc twice} around (24).

Rd 21 {1 Hdc, 2 Hdc Tog} around (16).

Rd 22 2 Hdc Tog around (8).

Finish stuffing a bit more if necessary.

Sl St in next stitch. Fasten off. Leave a tail long enough to weave through and tighten the 8 remaining stitches. Tie off and hide the end.

ARMS AND LEGS (MAKE 4)

Using H hook and brown yarn, Ch 2.

Rd 1 6 Hdc in second Ch from hook (6).

Rd 2 2 Hdc in each stitch around (12).

Rd 3–8 1 Hdc in each stitch around (12).

Sc in next stitch, Sl St in next stitch. Fasten off and leave a tail for sewing. Stuff, sew closed, and then sew the limbs to the body.

MUZZLE

Use H hook and brown yarn.

Rd 1 6 Sc in second Ch from hook (6).

Rd 2 2 Sc in each stitch around (12).

Rd 3 {1 Sc, 2 Sc} around (18).

Rd 4-5 1 Sc in each stitch around (18).

Sl St in next stitch. Fasten off and leave a tail for sewing. Stuff.

Sew the muzzle to the front of the head.

Embroider a nose and mouth on the muzzle. Embroider eyes above the muzzle.

EARS (MAKE 2)

1 Using H hook and brown yarn, Ch 5.

2 Sc in second Ch from hook.

3 Hdc, Dc in next stitch.

4 Dc, Hdc in next stitch.

5 Sc in last stitch.

6 Fasten off, leaving a long tail for sewing.

7 Sew the ears on top of the head, slightly curved inward.

HELMET

Use H hook and gray yarn. The Ch spaces in round 2 are where the bear's ears stick out. Ch 3 on rounds 2 through 4 count as a Dc.

Ch 3.

Rd 1 12 Dc in third Ch from hook, Sl St in top of first Dc.

Rd 2 Ch 2, (Dc, Ch1, Dc) in first stitch, {1 Dc, 2 Dc} twice, Dc in next stitch, (Dc, Ch 1, Dc) in next stitch, {1 Dc, 2 Dc} twice, Dc in next stitch, Sl St in first Dc, Sl St in next 2 stitches, Ch 3, turn (18).

Rd 3 Dc in same stitch and in next 11 stitches, 2 Dc in next stitch, Ch 3, turn (15).

Rd 4 Dc in same stitch and in next 13 stitches, 2 Dc in next stitch, Ch 1.

Rd 5 Rev Sc all the way around.

HELMET CREST

Ch 8. Sc, Hdc, Dc, 3 Dc, Hdc, Sc, Sl St. Fasten off, leaving a long tail for sewing to the top of the helmet.

SWORD

Using F hook and white yarn, Ch 2.

Rd 1 4 Sc in second Ch from hook.

Rd 2–8 1 Sc in each stitch around.

Rd 9 Sc 2 Tog. Twice.

Rd 10 Sc 2 Tog.

Fasten off and weave in the end.

With the white yarn on the needle, sew the sword to the end of the arm, creating a cross guard for the sword.

SHIELD

Using H hook and gray yarn, Ch 2.

Rd 1 6 Sc in second Ch from hook (6).

Rd 2 2 Sc in each stitch (12).

Rd 3 Sc in next 3 stitches, (Hdc, Dc, Hdc in next stitch), Sc in next 2 stitches, (Hdc, Dc, Hdc in next stitch), Sc in next 4 stitches, (Hdc, Dc, Hdc in next stitch) Sc in next stitch, Sl St in next stitch.

Fasten off and weave in the end.

Using white yarn, sew the shield to the end of the other arm, making an X in center of the shield.

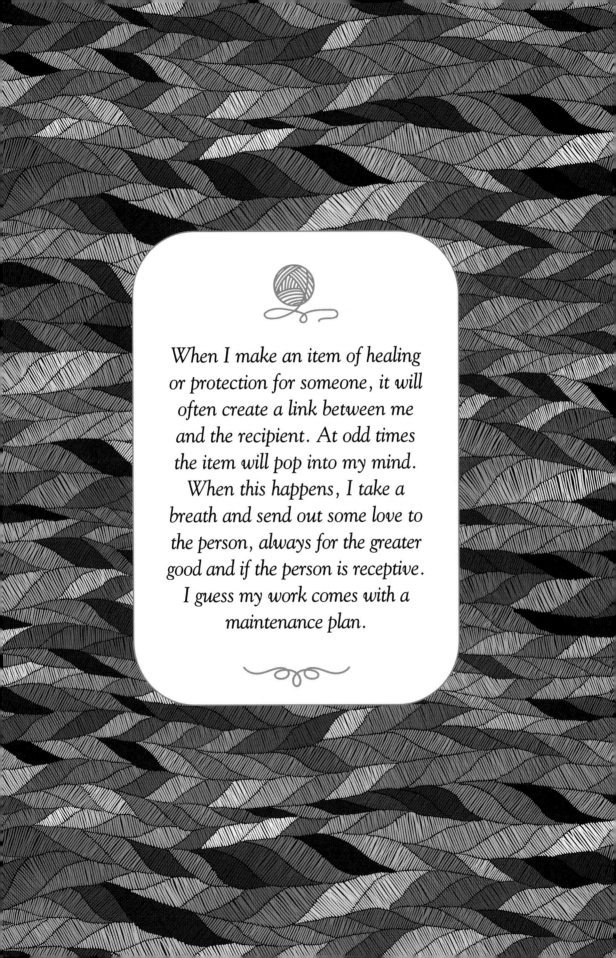

When I make an item of healing or protection for someone, it will often create a link between me and the recipient. At odd times the item will pop into my mind. When this happens, I take a breath and send out some love to the person, always for the greater good and if the person is receptive. I guess my work comes with a maintenance plan.

Chapter 12

Rites of Passage

As we go through our lives, we reach milestones that we should celebrate and reflect on. Fiber Magick can help record these rites of passage with a keepsake or tool for the occasion. A rite of passage is a ritual or ceremony to celebrate and mark the moving from one phase of life to the next. Change is not always easy, even if we are looking forward to what is coming. Rites of passage ease us over the threshold into the next phase and help us understand and embrace our new status.

Birthdays

Young ones cannot wait till they are twelve or eighteen or twenty-one because of the associated privileges. The novelty can wear thin as privileges become responsibilities. Thirty? Forty? When exactly do we feel the need to apply the brakes when it comes to the celebrating of a birthday? In any case, no matter how old we are, another trip around the sun is a privilege in itself and should be celebrated. Including an activity for the guests at the party can make it special. The gang can create a group Fiber Magick project. Make a garland of wishes for the birthday person to wear as a headband, necklace, or belt for the rest of the party.

Garland of Wishes

- -

Cut the length of ribbon long enough to be knotted as many times as you have guests and still have enough length on both ends to be tied around the birthday person's neck or waist. Make it a nice, soft ribbon that will be comfortable on the forehead or hang nicely as a necklace or belt.

Have a selection of beads for the guests to choose from. Make it a good variety of colors and shapes for a variety of wishes. When you tie them to the ribbon, you can either start at one end and work to the other or start in the middle and work outward to both ends. The knots will be holding the beads in place, so you may want to supervise just a little bit to get the beads close enough together so that everyone can get their bead on the ribbon.

This project could definitely translate into a baby shower activity. It is also perfect for a couple at their engagement or anniversary party. It is good for anytime, really, when there are wishes to be given and hopefully cake.

SKILL LEVEL
Beginner

FINISHED SIZE
Varies

YOU WILL NEED
Length of ribbon in the appropriate color
Beads that will slide on the ribbon

INSTRUCTIONS
Allow each guest to choose a bead. Instruct them to hold it in their hand and think of a wish for the birthday person. Give them a minute or two to visualize this wish, and then ask them one by one to come up, place their bead on the ribbon, and tie a knot to secure it.

When all the wishes have been tied and the birthday person is wearing their crown or necklace, that is the best time for singing and letting the birthday person blow out their candles. That way, the birthday person gets to add their wish to everyone else's.

Handfasting

In place of a traditional marriage ceremony, some opt for a handfasting. The commitment is sometimes viewed as temporary. A trial period of the arrangement may end on an agreed date, usually a year and a day from the ceremony. Then if both parties are agreeable, a more permanent ceremony can be performed. You may also choose a handfasting to renew vows at milestone anniversaries and make the cords silver for twenty-five years or gold for fifty.

Handfastings are a fine place to include some Fiber Magick. What better way to "tie the knot," so to speak. There is much emphasis on the knot itself when planning a handfasting. Couples and selected family members practice for weeks beforehand to get it right.

But let us think for a while about the cord itself. That's where the most powerful Fiber Magick could be performed. It can be done as with any true knot magick at the best time, under the best conditions, with everyone adding their blessing to it. Then, at the actual ceremony this cord could be draped around and possibly tied in a simple knot underneath the couple's hands.

Handfasting Cords

SKILL LEVEL
Beginner
Advanced if using I cord

FINISHED SIZE
6'

YOU WILL NEED
4 oz (208 yds) of 4-ply
   yarn (if making
   I cord) or 6 yds of
   1"-wide silk or satin
   ribbon
4 oz (208 yds) of
   chunky yarn
4 oz (208 yds) of super
   chunky yarn
Crochet hooks in size
   H/8 5.00 mm and
   J/10 6.00 mm
9 pearl beads
Sewing needle and
   thread
Embellishments

The strands that you choose or choose to create should reflect the couple being handfasted. If you are making this cord for someone else, you should conduct an interview unless you know them well. It would be fine for each partner to design a strand and then pick one out together. The braiding of the cords would represent their lives coming together and becoming intertwined. This cord can be coiled and placed in a shadow box after the ceremony for a very unique remembrance. Take it out every year on your anniversary to relive the moment and renew those vows.

When crocheting the I cord, it is very important to pinch the two loops that you take off your hook so they do not slip out as you pull the yarn through the previous one. This will take some practice and may seem tedious at first, but once you get the hang of it, you can focus on the meditative properties of the exercise. Chanting in multiples of three adds to the energy: Maiden, Mother, Crone; love, peace, and joy; or today, tomorrow, and always. Put on some music in the rhythm that matches your skill level and you will have a six-foot strand done in no time.

INSTRUCTIONS

1 Use 4-ply yarn and the H hook to create a 6-foot length of I cord as described below, or or use 1-inch wide ribbon and the J hook to crochet a chain 6 feet in length.

2 Cut 3 9-inch lengths of chunky yarn and braid them together to create a 6-foot length of braided cord.

3 Use very chunky yarn and the J hook to crochet a chain 6 feet in length.

4 Place the three strands on a flat surface, side by side, matching the ends.

5 Find the center of the length and sew three beads across the three strands. Sew each bead to one cord, but use a single thread so that the strands are connected. The strands will still lie flat side by side but be connected at this point.

6 Measure 9 inches out from the center in both directions and sew 3 more beads at those points in the same way.

7 Embellish as desired.

HOW TO CROCHET I CORD

1 Ch 3 in the 4-ply yarn with an H hook.

2 Insert hook into second Ch from hook, Yo, pull through.

3 Insert hook into third Ch from hook, Yo, pull through.

4 {Take loops 2 and 3 off hook, pinch them tight.

5 Yo, pull through loop.

6 Insert hook into loop 2, Yo, pull through.

7 Insert hook into loop 3, Yo, pull through}.

8 Repeat between { } until the I cord is 6 feet long.

Baby Blessings

The birth of a child is a momentous occasion. Most traditions have ceremonies to introduce the new one to the community. You may choose to invite family and friends over a month or two after the birth to tell them of your experience and explain the significance of the baby's name.

When you are invited to a gathering such as this, it is usually appropriate to bring a gift with some spiritual meaning for the baby. The warrior bear outlined in the previous chapter (see page 242) would be an excellent choice. If time is a factor, you could make the ward frame, also in the previous chapter (see page 238), in colors to match your best wishes for the baby.

Baby Blanket

There is always an inclination to make baby things in pastels, pink for girls and blue for boys. New information about the gender identification spectrum makes all this quite archaic. When I'm asked about baby gifts now, I suggest high-contrast colors such as red, white, and black. The baby can see them. It stimulates the brain, which is way more important than the genitals, in my way of thinking. The classic granny square is ideal for creating patterns with blocks of color.

SKILL LEVEL
Intermediate

FINISHED SIZE
38" × 38"

YOU WILL NEED
7 oz (364 yds) of yarn
    in color A
7 oz (364 yds) of yarn
    in color B
7 oz (364 yds) of yarn
    in color C
Crochet hook size I/9
    5.50 mm
Yarn needle

INSTRUCTIONS
Make 12 granny squares of each color:

Ch 5, Sl St in first Ch to form ring.

Rd 1 Ch 3, 2 Dc in ring, {Ch 2, 3 Dc in ring} 3 times, Ch 2, Sl St in top of Ch 3. Ch 3 and turn.

Rd 2 2 Dc, Ch 2, 3 Dc in first Ch Sp (corner), {Ch 2, (3 Dc, Ch 2, 3 Dc) in next Ch Sp} 3 times, Ch 2, Sl St in top of Ch 3. Ch 3 and turn.

Rd 3 2 Dc in Ch space, Ch 2, (3 Dc, Ch 2, 3 Dc) in next Ch Sp, {Ch 2, 3 Dc in next Ch Sp, Ch 2, (3 Dc, Ch 2, 3 Dc) in next Ch Sp} 3 times, Ch 2, Sl St in top of Ch 3. Ch 3 and turn.

Rd 4 Dc in next 5 stitches, (3 Dc, Ch 2, 3 Dc) in next Ch Sp, {Dc in next 13 St, (3 Dc, Ch 2, 3 Dc) in next Ch Sp} 3 times, Dc in next 8 stitches, Sl St in top of Ch 3.

Fasten off.

JOINING
Sides of these squares are reversable. Match edges stitch to stitch and whip stitch the inner loops together. Make an extra stitch in all the corners to prevent gaps. This is my suggested pattern placement:

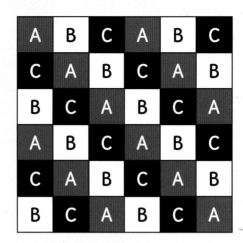

BORDER

1 Dc in each stitch around with (3 Dc, Ch 2, 3 Dc) in each corner space.

2 Rev Sc in each stitch around.

3 Perform the project blessing ritual on page 17.

Self-Dedication or "Year and a Day"

At some point on a spiritual path a person may feel moved to make it official. If one becomes part of a group, there will be a ceremony. My group, Moonpath CUUPS, celebrates attendees' first anniversary with a year and a day ceremony. When I celebrated my year and a day, way back when, the high priest tied a knot in the end of a very thick cord like the type used in upholstery. He had me step on the knot while he pulled it up over the top of my head. He then tied a second knot at that point and cut it off. He handed it to me and declared it was "my measure" that I was to give to the Goddess. That was such great symbolism well befitting my future practice of Fiber Magick.

That "measure" of cord can be used to close a robe and be secured with a pin made with a Fiber Magick star sigil.

Fiber Magick Star Sigil

- -

This sigil was inspired by my logo, which is a ball of yarn spiraling up into a pentagram. Imagine that happening for real as you make a ball of yarn become a star that ends in a spiral. The Sc is for healing waters, and five suggests a journey or change. Farewell on your Fiber Magick path.

SKILL LEVEL
Intermediate

FINISHED SIZE
4"

YOU WILL NEED
6 yds of 4-ply yarn in
desired color
Crochet hook size H/8
5.00 mm
Sew-on pin

INSTRUCTIONS

Ch 2.

Rd 1 5 Sc in second Ch from hook (5).

Rd 2 2 Sc in each stitch around (10).

Rd 3 Sl St in next stitch, {Ch 1, Sc in same stitch, Ch 2, Dc in next stitch, picot, place 3 Sc evenly down the side of the Dc, Sl St in next stitch} 5 times to create star points.

Work surface stitches in a spiral to the center of the star.

Fasten off, weave in the end, and sew on the pin back.

Attach the star to your "measure."

CHARGING

The star will charge and continue collecting energy when worn during ritual and spells.

Becoming a Maiden or Warrior

Most cultures and traditions have ceremonies that usher young people into adulthood. This small pouch would be appreciated as a small token to keep a treasure or necessity. If you are celebrating your daughter's menarche, this pouch could hold tampons. If your young person is ready to help tend the ritual fire, use this pouch for a fire-starting kit. Make the receiving of this personal pouch feel like a step closer to adulthood.

Personal Pouch

- -

This pouch is worked in joined rounds, not a spiral. Join the last stitch of each round to the first with a Sl St. You may choose to change colors every row or as desired.

SKILL LEVEL
Beginner

FINISHED SIZE
4" × 5"

YOU WILL NEED
2 oz (104 yds) of 4-ply
   cotton yarn
Crochet hook size H/8
   5.00 mm
½" button
Needle
Thread

INSTRUCTIONS

Ch 2.

Rd 1 6 Sc in second Ch from hook, join (6).

Rd 2 Ch 1. 2 Sc in each stitch around, join (12).

Rd 3 Ch 1, {1 Sc, 2 Sc} around, join (18).

Rd 4 Ch 1, {1 Sc twice, 2 Sc} around, join (24).

Rd 5–15 Ch 1, {1 Sc 3 times, 2 Sc} around, join (30).

Row 16 Ch 1, 1 Sc in next 15 stitches. Ch 1, turn.

Row 17 2 Sc Tog, 1 Sc 11 times, 2 Sc Tog, Ch 1, turn (13).

Row 18 2 Sc Tog, 1 Sc 9 times, 2 Sc Tog, Ch 1, turn. (11).

Row 19 2 Sc Tog, 1 Sc 7 times, 2 Sc Tog, Ch 1, turn. (9).

Row 20 2 Sc Tog, 1 Sc 5 times, 2 Sc Tog, Ch 1, turn. (7).

Row 21 2 Sc Tog, 1 Sc 3 times, 2 Sc Tog, Ch 1, turn. (5).

Row 22 2 Sc Tog, 1 Sc in next stitch. 2 Sc Tog, Ch 1, turn (3).

BORDER

1 Work Rev Sc stitches down the side of the flap, around the edge of the pouch opening, and back up other side of flap. Make the last Sl St in the third stitch of row 22. Ch 5. Slip stitch into first stitch of row 22.

2 Fasten off but leave the ends for the charging.

3 Sew the button on the front of the pouch.

DEDICATION AND CHARGING

1 Have the young person weave in the ends of the yarn.

2 Assist them to carry out the project blessing ritual on page 17.

3 At the end have them declare the purpose of their pouch.

Becoming a Parent

In the early stages of childcare, the baby needs so much of you that it is easy to lose sight of your own needs. A parent's pouch is a kind reminder for the new mom or dad. Decorate it to reflect the Mother, Father, God, or Goddess with appropriate colors and markings. Fill it with a few personal items to make sure the parent knows it's for them and not something else for the baby. Lipstick, cologne spray, or a protein bar may make a world of difference. Bless it with patience, good health, and organizational skills.

Parent's Pouch

This pouch starts with the zipper. Prepare the zipper by marking ¼-inch increments on both sides of the zipper opening. Make sure your markings line up across the zipper for a nicer look. The length of the zipper will determine the size of your finished pouch. Seven to nine inches would be a useful size that would still fit in the diaper bag.

You will be using a size 5 steel hook and size 3 cotton thread to make a foundation round on the zipper. It takes a bit of muscle to push the hook through the zipper material, but it can be done.

SKILL LEVEL
Intermediate

FINISHED SIZE
Zipper length × desired
depth

YOU WILL NEED
Crochet hook size 5
    steel
7"–9" zipper
1 oz (125 yds) size
    3 cotton crochet
    thread
Crochet hook size H/8
    5.00 mm
4 oz (208 yds) of 4-ply
    yarn
Yarn needle
Sewing needle
Thread
Embellishments

INSTRUCTIONS

1 Using the steel hook, attach your cotton thread to the zipper by inserting your hook at any marked point and pulling up a loop.

2 Make 1 Sc in each mark all the way around the zipper.

3 Sl St in first Sc made and fasten off.

4 Using the H hook, attach the yarn in any stitch and Sc in each stitch around, Ch 1, turn.

5 Continue rounds, 1 Sc in each stitch around, until your bag is the desired depth.

6 Fasten off and weave in the end.

7 Using the yarn needle and yarn, sew up the bottom of the pouch.

8 Make sure the ends of the zipper are tucked inside. Secure with a couple of stitches using the sewing needle and thread.

9 Embellish as desired.

DEDICATION AND BLESSING

Perform the project blessing ritual on page 17, and at the end declare,

May this pouch always hold what is needed at the proper time for (person's name). So mote it be.

Becoming a Crone or Sage

When exactly does a person become a sage or a crone? Ask three people and you may get three different answers to the question. You may get a number such as fifty or fifty-five, possibly even sixty, depending on the age of the person who's giving you the answer, and a short list of activities that are no longer appropriate. For the crone, you might get the technical answer of a woman who no longer bleeds.

I have a third answer, and it's more psychological than chronological: a crone or sage is a person who has come to grips with the fact that they are in the final stage of their earthly life. This fact does not scare them, for they can see beyond the veil and therefore know that there is nothing really "final" about it.

Enlightened people see their wisdom and spirit. They see that this is missing from this world and that the world suffers because of it. Encourage older members of the community to write down that wisdom and leave it for those smart enough to pay attention. Make a carrier for their Book of Shadows so they will have it with them when the muse strikes.

Book of Shadows Carrier

The pattern was made to cover a book measuring 7½ × 9¾ inches. This is the size of a composition notebook. If you use a blank book of different dimensions, you will have to adjust the number of chains you start with and the number of rows it takes to cover your book.

I used the moss stitch, which alternates Sc and Dc to create a moss-like texture. This stitch works best if you start with an odd number of chains. This way, you can begin each row with a Sc and end each row with a Dc. That eliminates the need to work with Ch 3 as a Dc.

As a decorative feature, you may want to make the wrap-around handles in a contrasting color. Any of the sigils from chapter 9 can be used to decorate the front. Keeping the book inserted while you are sewing the flaps, handles, closure, and embellishments prevents you from sewing through both thicknesses.

SKILL LEVEL
Beginner

FINISHED SIZE
10" × 8"

YOU WILL NEED
6 oz (312 yds) of 4-ply yarn
Crochet hook size H/8 5.00 mm
Yarn needle
Large button
Embellishments

INSTRUCTIONS

Ch 33.

Row 1 Sc in second Ch from hook, {1 Dc, 1 Sc} across (32).

Row 2–48 Ch 1 {1 Dc, 1 Sc} across (32).

Fasten off and weave in the end.

Fold the ends over 3 inches and sew the top and bottom to form pockets. Insert book as you would with a dust jacket.

FASTENING

Ch 7.

Row 1 Dc in third stitch from hook and next 4 Ch (5).

Row 2–5 Ch 2, Dc in same stitch and next 4 stitches (5).

Row 6 2 Dc Tog, 1 Dc, 2 Dc Tog (3).

Ch 8 and Sl St in third stitch in row.

Sew first two rows of the wide end to the back of the carrier. Keep the book inserted to prevent sewing the flap closed.

Sew the button on the front.

HANDLES

1 Chain 100.

2 Dc in fourth stitch from hook and each stitch across.

3 Sew the ends together, making sure you do not twist them.

4 Place the handle piece on a flat surface and lay the opened book carrier in the center with the handles extending evenly from both ends.

5 Pin in place so that the straps are evenly spaced from the top and bottom of the book carrier.

6 Sew the handles to the book carrier, taking care that you do not sew the flap shut.

7 Embellish as desired.

DEDICATION AND BLESSING

Leave the last end out to be weaved by the recipient. Explain the significance and let it be. A crone or sage will have their own way of consecrating it.

Funerals

Those who are remembered live.

In lieu of flowers, why not craft a keepsake for a friend or family member who has experienced a loss? Give them a little reminder to keep the memory alive. This small crocheted poppet can serve for a human or animal who has crossed the veil. With permission from the bereaved, you may offer to include a small vial of cremains inside.

Remembrance Poppet

The basic poppet will be the same for human or beast. The embellishments will be what makes it unique. Bits of felt can serve as ears and noses or make the crochet versions in the pattern.

Rosemary is an herb of remembrance, but you may choose to add others according to the recipient. Crystals and charms can be added to honor the individual. If you are making this poppet for a pet, adding their tags or a favorite treat would be nice.

The opening in the back of this poppet can be sewn up or left open so you can refresh the jar. I wanted to make this opening in the back so that the cremains could be placed inside with a ceremony. Dropping them in during the construction seemed disrespectful somehow.

SKILL LEVEL
Intermediate

FINISHED SIZE
6"

YOU WILL NEED
4 oz (208 yds) of 4-ply yarn
Crochet hook size H/8 5.00 mm
Yarn needle
2" circle of cardboard or plastic canvas to reinforce the bottom
2 oz glass jar, such as a baby food jar
Sprig of rosemary or herb of choice
Magickal components
Embellishments

INSTRUCTIONS

Ch 2.

Rd 1 8 Sc in second Ch from hook.

Rd 2 2 Sc in each stitch around (16).

Rd 3 {2 Sc, 1 Sc} around (24).

Rd 4 1 Sc in each stitch around (24).

Rd 5 In BLO, 1 Sc in each stitch around (24).

Rd 6–7 1 Sc in each stitch around (24).

Rd 8–14 Ch 1 and turn, 1 Sc in 24 stitches.

Rd 15–16 Do not turn. 1 Sc in each stitch around (24).

Rd 17 {1 Sc, 2 Sc Tog} around (16).

Rd 18 2 Sc Tog around (8).

Rd 19 1 Sc in each stitch around (8).

Rd 20 2 Sc in each stitch around (16).

Rd 21–25 1 Sc in each stitch around (16).

Rd 26 2 Sc Tog around (8).

Fasten off and weave the end to close.

Stuff the head only.

Embellish as desired.

Place the cardboard circle in the bottom and the filled jar inside.

Sew up the opening if desired.

PUPPY EARS (MAKE 2)

1 Ch 3.

2 1 Dc in third Ch from hook.

3 Ch 2, Sl St in same Ch as Dc.

4 Fasten off, leaving a long tail for sewing.

CAT EARS (MAKE 2)

1 Ch 4.

2 Sc in second Ch from hook.

3 2 Sc Tog, Ch 1, turn.

4 2 Sc Tog.

5 Fasten off, leaving a long tail for sewing.

MUZZLE

1 Ch 2.

2 6 Sc in second Ch from hook.

3 {2 Sc, 1 Sc} around.

4 Sl St in next stitch.

5 Fasten off, leaving a long tail for sewing.

ANGEL WINGS (MAKE 2)

Rd 1 Ch 7, work 1 Dc in the fifth Ch from the hook (the 4 skipped Ch count as 1 Dc, Ch 1), Ch 1, 1 Dc in the next Ch, Ch 1, 1 Dc in the last Ch, turn {4 Dc, 3 Ch 1 Sp}.

Rd 2 Ch 5 (counts as 1 Dc, Ch 2), 1 Dc in the Ch 1 Sp, Ch 2, 1 Dc in the next Ch 1 Sp, Ch 2, 1 Dc in the final Ch1 Sp, Ch 2, 1 Dc in the top of the third Ch {5 Dc, 4 Ch 2 Sp}.

Rd 3 Ch 6 (count as 1 Dc , Ch 3), {1 Dc in the Ch 2 Sp, Ch 3} 4 times, 1 Dc in the top of the third Ch. Turn. {6 Dc, 5 Ch 3 Sp}.

Rd 4 Ch 1, 1 Sl St in each stitch around.

Finish off, leaving a long tail.

Now take the yarn end on a yarn needle. Weave the needle in and out of the inside stitches down one side of the wing.

Pull the yarn needle through completely and pull snugly (to cinch the inside more tightly together), and weave back through again to secure the yarn end.

Finish off. Repeat for the second wing.

DEDICATION AND BLESSING

If there is no particular ritual according to your path, then the project blessing ritual on page 17 can be done, followed by a few personal words to or about the deceased.

Chapter 13

Holidays and Festivals

In this chapter we will use the skills we have learned in previous chapters to make a special project for each of the eight modern Pagan sabbats, plus one extra celebration. Each and every occasion in the year and in a life gives us reason to celebrate. There certainly is no shortage of opportunities to embellish these occasions with a little Fiber Magick. The sabbats bring a chance to remember and respect the ancestors and where we came from. They also provide an excellent reason for crafting.

Samhain Spiderweb

Celebrated from October 31 to November 1, this Gaelic festival is called the Witch's New Year. Samhain conjures up all the monstrous images of the secular Halloween but can also have a more somber feel. The veil is thin at this time, so we may be moved to remember or even be visited by our beloved dead. Our Samhain project can be used on an ancestor altar or placed at the table to represent a relative who is dining with us in spirit.

For the the crocheted mandala in chapter 7, we started in the center and worked out until we attached it to the hoop. This project starts on the hoop and works toward the center to form a web fit for any spider. Use the web to frame a picture of a relative who has passed through the veil.

SKILL LEVEL
Intermediate

FINISHED SIZE
9"

YOU WILL NEED
9" wooden embroidery hoop
2 oz (104 yds) of chunky white yarn
Crochet hook size H/8 5.00 mm
Yarn needle
2 fuzzy black pipe cleaners
1 black pony bead
Photos

INSTRUCTIONS

Separate hoop into 2 rings. Attach yarn to inside hoop with a Sc.

Rd 1 {Ch 5, Sc around hoop, Ch 5} 11 times, Sl St into the first Sc. Sl St in next 3 Ch.

Rd 2 Sc in same Ch, {Ch 8, Skip next Ch Sp, Sc in next Ch Sp, Ch 8} around, Sl St in first Sc, Sl St in next 4 Ch.

Rd 3 Sc in same Ch, {Ch 5, Sc in next Ch Sp, Ch 5} around, Sl St in first Sc. Sl St in next 3 Ch.

Rd 4 Sc in same Ch, {Ch 3, Sc in next Ch Sp, Ch 3} around, Sl St in first Sc. Sl St in next 2 Ch.

Rd 5 Sc in same Ch, Sc in each Ch 3 space around, Sl St in first Sc.

Fasten off and weave in the ends.

Cut the pipe cleaner in 4 equal pieces. Stick all 4 pieces through the pony bead. Splay out the legs and wrap one around any spoke of yarn on the web.

Display photos by tucking them into the web strands.

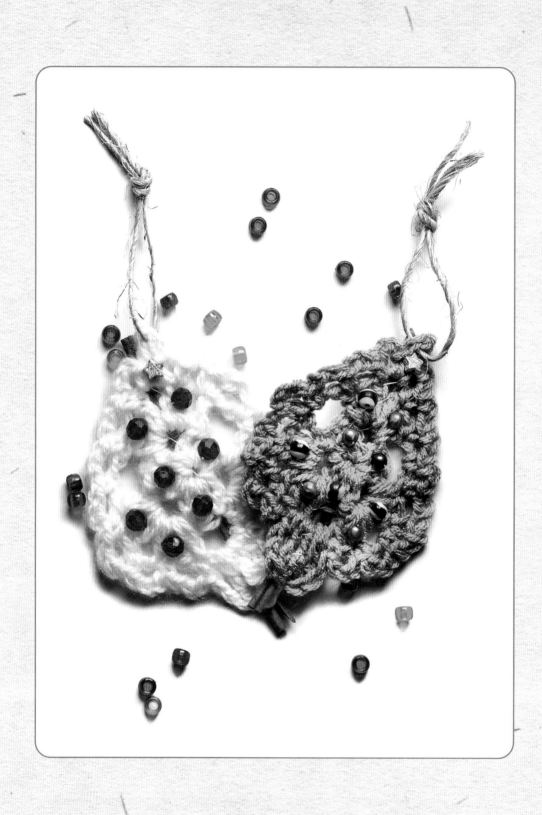

Yule Tree Ornament

Celebrated between December 20 and 22, this Germanic holiday welcomes the rebirth of the sun. Many traditions of Christmas are associated with Yule, such as decorating an evergreen tree to represent life amid the darkest months.

Use the granny square skill from the baby blanket on page 257, but only make three corners instead of four to make a nice little tree to hang on the big one. Reinforce with a cinnamon stick to add a trunk for stability and aroma.

SKILL LEVEL
Beginner

FINISHED SIZE
6"

YOU WILL NEED
15 yds of 4-ply yarn
Crochet hook size H/8
  5.00 mm
Twine for the hanger
  loop
Beads and
  embellishments
Sewing thread
Needle
6" cinnamon stick

INSTRUCTIONS

Ch 5, Sl St in first Ch to form ring.

Rd 1 Ch 3, 2 Dc in ring, Ch 2, 3 Dc in ring, Ch 2, 3 Dc in ring, Ch 2, Sl St in top of Ch 3. Ch 3 and turn.

Rd 2 (2 Dc, Ch 2, 3 Dc) in first Ch Sp, Ch 2, {(3 Dc, Ch 2, 3 Dc) in next Ch Sp, Ch 2} twice, Sl St in top of Ch 3. Do not turn.

Rd 3 Ch 1, Sc in same stitch , Ch 3, skip next stitch, Sc in next stitch, Ch 3, (Sc, picot, Sc) in Ch Sp, Ch 3, Sc in next stitch, {Ch 3, skip next stitch, Sc in next stitch} 6 times, Ch 2, 3 Trc in next Ch Sp, Ch 2, Sc in next stitch, {Ch 3, skip next stitch, Sc in next stitch} 4 times, Ch 3, Sl St in first Sc.

Fasten off and weave in the ends.

Tie twine through the picot for hanging.

Embellish with beads.

Whip stitch the tree onto the cinnamon stick down the center for support.

Imbolc New Sprouts Garland

- -

Celebrated on February 2, this Gaelic holiday reminds us that spring will come again. Go outside and look for those first sprouts poking through the frost and then come inside and make a garland for the floral crown on page 96.

Alternate turning and not turning the leaves so they point in toward opposite sides of the vine. Refer to chapter 7 for more information about stitches.

SKILL LEVEL
Beginner

FINISHED SIZE
Varies

YOU WILL NEED
15 yds of 4-ply yarn in
   spring colors
Crochet hook size H/8
   5.00 mm

INSTRUCTIONS

1 Ch 8.

2 2 Hdc cluster in third Ch from hook. To make a 2 Hdc cluster, {Yo, insert hook in Ch, Yo, pull up loop} twice (5 loops on hook), Yo, pull through all loops on hook.

3 Picot, Sl St in side of cluster, returning to base.

4 Ch 8.

5 2 Hdc cluster in third Ch from hook, picot, Sl St in side of cluster, returning to base. Turn the leaf upside down and make a surface Sl St in next Ch to cause leaf to turn the opposite way of the previous leaf.

6 Continue this pattern until the garland is the desired length.

Ostara Egg Basket

- -

Celebrated around March 20, spring is here! Celebrations will include bunnies and eggs and all symbols of fertility. The pastel colors of spring give this time a very lighthearted feel. It is a time to hope for future rewards. It is time to plant seeds, whether they are literal or figurative.

Ostara calls for colored eggs, and you can fuse them with intention by using any of the edible materials in the natural dyeing section starting on page 57. In small food-safe pots boil the plant material until the desired color is achieved, and then cook your eggs in this water. Serve your eggs in an Ostara egg basket.

Pastel colors would be appropriate for this basket, but jewel tones will show off the delicate colors of the eggs.

SKILL LEVEL
Intermediate

FINISHED SIZE
8" diameter

YOU WILL NEED
8 oz (384 yds) of
  chunky yarn
Crochet hooks size
  J/10 6.00 mm and
  D/3 3.25 mm
2 oz (250 yds) of
  cotton crochet
  thread size 3
Stitch marker
48 beads that will fit on
  the thread

INSTRUCTIONS

Ch 2.

Rd 1 8 Hdc in second Ch from hook, Sl St in first Hdc (8).

Rd 2 Ch 1, 2 Hdc in each stitch around, Sl St in first Hdc (16).

Rd 3 Ch 1 {2 Hdc, 1 Hdc} around, Sl St in first Hdc (24).

Rd 4 Ch 1, {2 Hdc, 1 Hdc twice} around, Sl St in first Hdc (32).

Rd 5 Ch 1, {2 Hdc, 1 Hdc 3 times} around, Sl St in first Hdc (40).

Rd 6 Ch 1, {2 Hdc, 1 Hdc 4 times} around, Sl St in first Hdc (48).

Rd 7 Ch 1, 1 Hdc in back loop in each stitch around, Sl St in first Hdc (48).

Rd 8–14 Ch 1, 1 Hdc in each stitch around, Sl St in first Hdc (48).

Fasten off and weave in the end.

String the beads on cotton crochet thread. Attach the thread to any stitch on Rd 14 with Sl St. Ch 3, bring up bead, Ch 4, Sl St in next stitch. {Ch 4, bring up bead, Ch 4, Sl St in next stitch} around.

Fasten off and weave in the end.

Fold over the edge so that the beads hang down.

Beltane Maypole Wand

Beltane takes place on May 1. This is when we dance the maypole and light the bonfire. Rituals are held to promote fertility. People and livestock jump or walk between fires to honor the sun and bring good luck. Beltane is a time to celebrate the coming together of the masculine and feminine energies and the fruit this will bring.

We can combine the two energies by crafting a Fiber Magick maypole wand of our own. The wooden crochet hook will represent the Lord and the crown of flowers and sparkles will represent the Lady. Use this Maypole as a wand while you dance around the Beltane fire, and then bring that energy into your next project. Make a special Beltane candle cozy with the pattern on page 133.

SKILL LEVEL
Beginner

FINISHED SIZE
Varies

YOU WILL NEED
Gold and silver paint
    markers
1 wooden afghan
    crochet hook size
    H/8 5.00 mm or
    larger
6 24" lengths of ¼"
    ribbon
1 pushpin
Small hammer
    (optional)
Hot glue and gun
Embellishments such
    as mini flowers and
    beads

INSTRUCTIONS

1 Use the markers to paint the hook.

2 Find the center of each ribbon and skewer them with the push pin.

3 Fan them out in all directions.

4 Press the push pin into the flat end of the hook. The hammer may help.

5 Hot glue mini flowers on the pushpin to finish off the look.

6 Dance with free abandon as if no one were watching, and add Beltane fire to your next project.

Litha Sun Weaving

Celebrated around June 21, the summer solstice is all about the Sun King in all his glory. The sun nourishes the earth, which is now heavily laden with grain, fruit, and flowers. It is time to frolic in the sun's warm glow, but beware fairy mischief as you celebrate the earth's bounty. The veil between the worlds is thin, and the Fey are frolicking too. On this longest day of the year, we celebrate the bounty but remember from this day forward the days will get shorter. Winter will come again, so let us be ready. But for now we will worship the sun. Include this variation of the nature weaving as outlined in chapter 6 on the Litha altar. Use all the sunny, fiery colors to create a representation of the sun. Use it on an altar or to bring the sunshine into your home. I like the way the stacked twigs create a 3D effect, but if you put a notch in one or two where they cross, they will lie almost flat.

SKILL LEVEL
Beginner

FINISHED SIZE
Varies

YOU WILL NEED
4 twigs of equal length
12" of thin wire
Materials for weaving,
    such as wool, yarn,
    ribbon, string,
    fabric strips, thread,
    grasses, leaves, or
    feathers
Embellishments
Yarn needle
Glue

INSTRUCTIONS

1 Place your twigs in a sunburst pattern, overlapping at the center.

2 Fix the center securely with wire by creating a figure eight pattern around each stick where they cross. The twigs should not move when you are weaving.

3 Start weaving your materials at the center. Tie a knot to secure the material and wrap it around each twig spoke, turning your work in a clockwise direction.

4 Continue weaving and watch your sunburst grow until it reaches the extent of your twigs. You can trim the twigs if you need.

5 Tuck or glue embellishments or plant material into the weaving. Attach something shiny to reflect the sun's energy in the center.

6 Tie a loop of yarn to one of the twigs for hanging and display your sunny sunburst to honor the Sun King's reign.

Lughnasadh Horned God Poppet

Celebrated on August 1, Lughnasadh is a festival to mark the annual wheat harvest and is the first harvest festival of the year. The product of our own labor comes together with the gifts of the Goddess and God, to provide us with food and life. Celebrate by baking a loaf of bread and serving it with some good butter, the color of the sun. The Horned God has sacrificed his body so that we may have our bread.

Use this poppet to add masculine energy to your altar. Make him in sunny colors to honor Lugh or harvest colors as befits the season.

SKILL LEVEL
Intermediate

FINISHED SIZE
16"

YOU WILL NEED
6 oz (312 yds) of 4-ply
    yarn in colors of the
    harvest
1 oz (52 yds) of 4-ply
    yarn in dark brown
1 brown pipe cleaner
Crochet hook size H/8
    5.00 mm
Stitch marker
Yarn needle
Small gold bead or
    button

INSTRUCTIONS

Ch 2.

Rd 1 9 Hdc in second Ch from hook (9).

Rd 2 1 Hdc in each stitch around (9).

Rd 3 {1 Hdc twice, 2 Hdc} in each stitch around (12).

Rd 4 1 Hdc in each stitch around (12).

Rd 5 {1 Hdc twice, 2 Hdc} in each stitch around (16).

Rd 6–7 1 Hdc in each stitch around (16).

Rd 8 {1 Hdc 3 times, 2 Hdc} in each stitch around (20).

Rd 9–10 1 Hdc in each stitch around (20).

Rd 11 {1 Hdc 3 times, 2 Hdc} in each stitch around (25).

Rd 12–13 1 Hdc in each stitch around (25).

Rd 14 {1 Hdc 4 times, 2 Hdc} in each stitch around (30).

Rd 15–16 1 Hdc in each stitch around (30).

Rd 17 {1 Hdc 4 times, 2 Hdc} in each stitch around (36).

Rd 18–20 1 Hdc in each stitch around (36).

Rd 21 {1 Hdc 5 times, 2 Hdc} in each stitch around (42).

Rd 22–24 1 Hdc in each stitch around (42).

Rd 25 {1 Hdc, 2 Hdc Tog} around (28).

Rd 26-27 1 Hdc in each stitch around (28).

Rd 28 2 Hdc Tog around (14).

Rd 29 1 Hdc in each stitch around (14).

Rd 30 2 Hdc in each stitch around (28).

Rd 31–34 1 Hdc in each stitch around (28).

Rd 35 2 Hdc Tog around (14).

Rd 36 2 Hdc Tog in each stitch around (7).

Fasten off, leaving a long end for weaving the last 7 stitches and pulling closed. Knot and pull the end inside the poppet.

Sew the gold bead or button on his forehead.

ARMS

Using the dark brown yarn, make folded arms on the front of the body. Use the gold bead as a guide to center the folded arms across chest.

1 Attach yarn at round 27, place 8 surface Sc down side of body to round 19. Making a 45-degree turn, place 9 surface Sc at a diagonal up and across body, fasten off, and pull the ends into the doll.

2 Attach yarn at round 27, place 8 surface Sc down opposite side of body to round 19. Making a 45-degree turn toward previous arm, place 9 surface Sc at a diagonal up and across body, crossing the arms on his chest, fasten off, and pull the ends into the doll.

ANTLERS

1 Insert the pipe cleaner through the top of the head at round 35.

2 Bend each end of the pipe cleaner over and pinch.

3 Attach yarn with Sl St over pipe cleaner close to head (push stitches toward head as you go to thoroughly cover pipe cleaner).

4 6 Sc over pipe cleaner, Ch 3, Sl St back in next 2 Ch, 6 Sc over pipe cleaner, {Ch 5, Sl St back in next 4 Ch}. Repeat { } twice more. Fasten off, leaving a tail for sewing. Weave it back through your work until you get to the folded end of the pipe cleaner, insert yarn needle through the end, tighten and stitch to secure, and cut off extra yarn.

5 Repeat step 4 to cover the other end of the pipe cleaner for the opposite antler.

Mabon Mug Cozy

- -

Celebrated around September 21, the second harvest conjures up images of abundance. Cornucopias of squash and pumpkins. Mugs of hot beverages laced with the heady spices of autumn. Keep the cider warm with a cozy adorned with any of the Fiber Magick crocheted sigils. Mix up some homemade pumpkin spice to add the magick to the inside of the mug as well.

This mug cozy uses the same technique as for the basic witch's hatband on page 146 but this time with Sc for the element of water, the first ingredient in all the yummiest beverages.

SKILL LEVEL
Beginner

FINISHED SIZE
Fits a 12-oz mug

YOU WILL NEED
2 oz (108 yds) of 4-ply yarn

Crochet hook size H/8 5.00 mm

Crocheted sigil or other embellishment

INSTRUCTIONS

Ch 13.

Row 1 Sc in second Ch from hook, Sc across, Ch 1 and turn (12).

Row 2 Sc across in BLO (12).

Row 3–30 Repeat row 2 (12).

Hold short ends together and make 1 Sl St in first stitch, Sc in same stitch, Ch 1.

Working around the top edge of cozy Sc, Ch 1 in each groove around (15 Sc, 15 Ch).

Fasten off and repeat for the bottom edge of cozy.

Fasten off, weave in the ends, and embellish.

The cozy fits over the mug like a sweater with the opening for the handle. Sew up the opening to use it on a thermal cup.

Pumpkin Spice for Your Cup

This mixture is perfect for pies, cakes, and coffee of course, but remember a pinch added to a poppet or spell bag will also bring the desired results. Just the thought of a pumpkin spice teddy bear makes me happy.

Cinnamon brings abundance and promotes healing and love. It offers protection and ensures success. We should be sprinkling a bit of cinnamon on everything!

Ginger is for love and money. It is also strong enough to protect both. Stir it vigorously into that cinnamon.

Adding allspice attracts a little more money, which never hurts. It also adds healing.

Nutmeg will bring clarity. We want to use all this abundance and success in useful ways and always for the greater good.

Cloves will draw friendships and raise your vibrations.

Stir the mixture clockwise to further raise those vibrations. This recipe yields three tablespoons.

You Will Need

4 teaspoons of ground cinnamon
2 teaspoons of ground ginger
1 teaspoon of ground allspice
1 teaspoon of ground nutmeg
1 teaspoon of ground cloves

Instructions

1 Mix the ingredients in a bowl and store the blend in an airtight container.

2 After you make this recipe and taste it, you can adjust the spices to suit your taste.

Pagan Pride Ribbon

Pagan Pride Days, annual gatherings that aim to show a positive public image of Paganism, are held all across the country, usually on or near the autumn equinox. Many different Pagan paths are represented, and proceeds will go to any number of charities according to the needs of the area. Celebrations may include workshops, rituals, and demonstrations all open to the public. Openly sharing may serve to take away some of the stigma associated with Paganism due to more mainstream beliefs.

The Pagan Pride ribbon is purple with a pentagram where it crosses. Wouldn't it also be great to make several with different symbols of faith for everyone to take pride in their paths while celebrating each other's beliefs?

SKILL LEVEL
Beginner

FINISHED SIZE
6"

YOU WILL NEED
1 oz (52 yds) of purple 4-ply yarn
Crochet hook size H/8 5.00 mm
Yarn needle
Charm of the symbol of your choice

INSTRUCTIONS

Ch 31.

Row 1 Sc in first 12 Ch, 2 Sc in each of next 6 Ch, Sc in last 12 Ch.

Row 2 Ch 1, Sc in first 12 stitches, {2 Sc, 1 Sc} 6 times, 1 Sc in each of remaining 12 stitches.

Row 3 Ch 1, Sc in first 12 stitches, {2 Sc, 1 Sc twice} 6 times, 1 Sc in each of remaining 12 stitches.

Rev Sc around the entire piece, then fasten off.

Arrange the curved strip into the ribbon shape. Using a yarn needle and piece of yarn, sew the ribbon together where the "legs" cross, adding a charm at the same time.

Conclusion

Layers of intention through the correspondences of sympathetic magick bring the most simple crafting project to life. No matter what your fiber hobby may be, it can be incorporated into your magickal practice. Turning basic knot magick into an art form and adding magickal flair to your Craft and crafting is what makes Fiber Magick an enhancement to any path.

I hope this book has whetted your appetite for some crafting and filled your head with ideas on how to bring it into your personal spirituality. I also hope you had some fun along the way.

As you allow your imagination to take you to new heights of creativity, you will find your visualization skills improve. Improved visualization will take you to new heights in magick. There are no limits to where this will take you. May you see all your dreams come true!

Stay crafty,

Opal Luna

Appendix:
Correspondences

Colors

Red: The element of fire, sexual energy, passionate love, anger, heat, confidence and courage, strength, energy, protection against being attacked

Pink: Romantic love, friendship, warm family, goodness, peace, sweetness, forgiveness, sleep

Orange: Joy and laughter, creativity, major changes, encouragement, confidence, warmth, enthusiasm, activity, energy, the harvest, fertility, attracting what you need or want

Yellow: The element of air, ideas, mental clarity, strengthening the intellect, knowledge, studying, business ventures, counseling, happiness, optimism

Green: The element of earth, wealth and money, prosperity, luck, success and achievement, healing and health, growth, earth magick, nature and garden spells, fertility, marriage, balancing an unstable situation

Blue: The element of water, peace, tranquility, emotions, loyalty, healing relationships

Purple: Intuition, spirituality, spiritual power and development, spiritual healing, invoking spirits, higher psychic ability, connecting with higher realms, wisdom, dream work, general protection, success, progress, fame and promotion, happiness

Brown: The element of earth, earth elementals, communicating with nature spirits, grounding, balance, earth energies, hearth, home

Black: Absorption and removal of negativity, repelling dark magick, banishing, uncrossing, releasing, breaking up blocks, removing hexes, letting go, binding

White: Neutral color that can be used for anything; cleansing, truth, purity, protection

Gray: Fairy magick and communicating with fairy realms, vision quests, veiling, cancellation, hesitation, balance through compromise

Gold: The sun, solar magick, masculinity, victory, overcoming, honor, ambition, success, power, prosperity, higher intuition, good fortune, quick money

Silver: The moon, moon magick, femininity, psychic development, divination, astral work, insight

Days of the Week

Sunday: Personal achievements

Monday: Emotional situations

Tuesday: Facing a challenge

Wednesday: Making a change

Thursday: Protection during travel, health

Friday: Matters of the heart

Saturday: Protection, banishing

Divine Numbers

1: Aphrodite, Apollo, Diana

2: Ceres, Freya, Venus

3: Cronos, Hecate, Pluto, Saturn

4: YHVH, Jupiter, Odin, Zeus

5: Dionysus, Ishtar, Mars, Thor

6: Athena, Bacchus, Hermes

7: Frigg, Minerva, Yemaya

8: Mercury, Gaia, Hera

9: Juno, Luna, the All-Father

10: Atlas, Uranus

11: Neptune, Poseidon

12: Janus

13: Hades, Pluto

Appendix: Correspondences

Fabrics

TYPE	ELEMENT	SIGN	CORRESPONDENCES
Bamboo	Water	Pisces	Protection, luck, hex-breaking, wishes
Canvas	Earth	Taurus	Creativity, new beginnings, potential, possibilities
Cashmere	Earth	Virgo	Comfort, warmth, luxury
Chiffon	Air	Aquarius	Femininity, delicacy, vulnerability, elegance
Cotton	Earth	Virgo	Healing, luck, protection; burn to attract rain
Denim	Earth	Taurus	Ruggedness, durability, labor, working, independence, rebellion
Felt	Earth	Capricorn	Protection, good luck, wealth (white felt), sacrifice, strength
Flannel	Earth	Cancer	Comfort, relaxation, warmth; use for mojo bags
Flax	Earth	Capricorn	Prosperity, gift of the gods
Gauze	Air	Gemini	Wealth, healing
Hemp	Spirit	(None)	Cleanses, heals, increases perception, magnifies and amplifies any magickal work. In my opinion, hemp could save the world. It can be used as cloth, rope, food, fuel—you name it. Using it in your magick could add a glimmer of hope.
Lace	Fire	Sagittarius	Sacredness, rite of passage, femininity, privilege, sensuality, sexuality, duality
Lamé	Fire	Leo	Luxury, wealth, royalty, sun, moon
Leather	Earth	Taurus	Protection, covering, animals, instinct
Linen	Spirit	(None)	Righteousness, purity, rest, elegance, luxury, sophistication
Satin	Fire	Libra	Luster, sensuality, shine, love

Appendix: Correspondences

TYPE	ELEMENT	SIGN	CORRESPONDENCES
Silk	Water	Scorpio	Occult properties, insulation from random energy, psychic contamination, preventing spirits from seeing you (your own cloak of invisibility)
Velvet	Fire	Leo	Distinction, honor, sensuality, emotions, royalty, leadership
Voile	Air	Libra	Secrets, unveiling, hidden, wedding
Wool	Earth	Aries	Hope, renewal, spinning, women's crafts, durability, comfort, warmth; comes from sheep, which correspond with determination

Flowers

African Violet: Protection

Chrysanthemum: Mental clarity

Clover: Abundance

Dandelion: Wishes

Hibiscus: Independence

Lily: Peace

Lotus: Creative flow

Magnolia: Goddess wisdom

Marigold: Healing

Morning Glory: Awakening

Pansy: Stress relief

Poppy: Calm energy

Rose: Love

Herbs, Spices, and Resins

Allspice: Money attraction, love, extra physical energy

Anise: Used to help ward off the evil eye, find happiness, and stimulate psychic ability

Apple: Peace of mind, relaxation, love, wisdom

Appendix: Correspondences

Basil: Love, exorcism, wealth, sympathy, protection; dispelling confusion, fears, and weakness; driving off hostile spirits

Black Pepper: Banishing, protection, passion, warding against magickal attacks

Caraway: Protection, health, and anti-theft

Cayenne: Dealing with separations or divorce, cleansing, purification, repelling negativity, speeding up the effects of any mixture to which it is added

Cedar: Confidence, purification, protection, speeding up healing, spirituality

Chamomile: Psychic awareness, intuition, yin

Cinnamon: Love, work, lust, dispelling negative energy, spirituality, success, healing, protection, power, love, luck, strength, prosperity, yang

Clove: Spiritual vibrations, clairvoyance, memory, protection, courage, money, love, purification

Coffee: Dispelling nightmares and negative thoughts, overcoming internal blockages, peace of mind, grounding

Cypress: Blessings, consecrations, healing, easing pain of loss, yin

Dill: Money, protection, luck, lust

Dragon's Blood: Love, protection, exorcism, sexual potency

Eucalyptus: Healing, depression relief, illness, yin

Fennel: Guarding against evil, strength, protection, purification

Flax Seed: Money, healing

Frankincense: Creating sacred space, positive vibrations, purification, protection, spirituality, love, concentration, meditation, spiritual states

Gardenia: Peace, love, healing

Garlic: Protection, health, banishing

Geranium: Protection, harmony, well-being, joy, happiness, yin

Ginger: Love, courage, attracting money, adventure and new experiences, sensuality, sexuality, personal confidence, prosperity, success, yang

Jasmine: Strength in spiritual matters, love, money

Juniper: Exorcism, protection, healing, love, yang

Lemon: Evoking protective spirits, lemon

Lotus: Inner peace and outer harmony

Appendix: Correspondences

Mint: Success, purification, concentration, energy, communication, vitality

Musk: Prosperity, courage, sensuality

Myrrh: Guarding against evil, peace, understanding, yang

Nag Champa: Enhancing energies into harmonious balance, clearing, cleansing

Nutmeg: Attracting money, prosperity, bringing luck, protection, breaking hexes

Orange: Harmony, raising power

Parsley: Calming and protecting the home

Patchouli: Attracting lusty ventures, evoking memories, yang

Pine: Prosperity, ridding an area of spiritual interference, cleansing, decluttering

Rose: Clarity in matters of the heart, picking up the spirit, soothing the angered soul, relaxing the space, yin

Rosemary: Protection, healing, increasing intellectual powers, mental clarity, yang

Rue: Banishing, health, revealing evil

Sage: Clearing, cleansing, removing negative energy, healing, spirituality, yang

Salt: Cleansing, clearing, prosperity, protection

Sandalwood: Moon energy, shielding, sealing an entrance, protection

Strawberry: Luck, friendship

Thyme: Health, healing, purification, yang

Vanilla: Emotional growth, pleasure, vitalizing energy, good fortune

Metals

Copper: Venus, love spells, conducting energy, health, balance, good foundations

Gold: The sun, the God, strength, leadership, power, authority, wealth

Iron: Mars, strength, safety, protection from harmful spirits, power, courage

Lead: The earth, practicality, meditation, stability, grounding

Silver: The moon, the Goddess, insight, dreams, psychic awareness, creativity

Tin: Jupiter, success, abundance

Natural Dyes

MATERIAL	COLOR	INTENTIONS
Avocado (skin and seed)	Light pink	Beauty, love
Bamboo	Turkey red	Breaking a hex or bringing some luck
Beets	Deep red	Love spells
Black tea	Brown	Courage
Blackberries, blueberries	Strong purple	Work with the Fey, money, healing
Carrot	Orange	Lust and fertility
Coffee grounds	Beige	Peace of mind, grounding
Concentrated grape juice	Purple	Fertility, money, mental powers
Curry powder or turmeric	Gold	Purification
Eucalyptus (all parts, including leaves and bark)	Beautiful shades of tan, deep rust red, yellow, green, orange, and chocolate brown	Clarity, healing, protection
Geranium	Blue-gray	Health, protection
Lavender (flower)	Pink	Love, peace
Onion, red (skin, fresh or dried)	Reddish orange	Prophetic dreams
Onion, yellow (skin, fresh or dried)	Burnt orange	Protection
Paprika	Red or pink	Adding energy to any spell or mixture
Peppermint	Dark khaki green color	Psychic powers, purification

MATERIAL	COLOR	INTENTIONS
Rose (red)	Brilliant pink (and with a little mint and some lemon juice to activate the alkaloids, you can make both the dye and a very tasty pink lemonade)	Love, peace
Spinach	Leaf green	Money
Tea bags	Tan to warm brown	Courage, strength
Walnut (hulls)	Deep brown to black (wear gloves)	Mental abilities, wishes

Numbers

0: Potential

1: Self-awareness

2: Balance, duality

3: Emphasis

4: Stability, grounding

5: Journeys, changes

6: Insight, clarity

7: Luck, chance

8: Success, abundance

9: Completion

10: Maturity

Power Shapes

Circle: Oneness, wholeness, sacred space

Pentagram: The five elements, protection

Rectangle: Stable growth, moving forward

Spiral: Unfurling of that which is hidden

Square: Earth, stability

Triangle: Trinity, mind-body-spirit, Maiden-Mother-Crone

Stones

Agate: Balance, emotional strength, self-confidence

Amazonite: Balanced energy, harmony, universal love, attracting money

Amber: Protection, thwarting hexes, luck

Amethyst: Spirituality, meditation, calming fears, reducing stress, dispelling anger and negativity, relieving depression

Aquamarine: Peace, happiness, love, joy, soothing and calming emotions, creativity, clarity, mental awareness

Aventurine: Prosperity, abundance, fertility

Carnelian: Healing of sacral chakra, creativity, talent, easing indecision and procrastination, courage

Citrine: Good luck, creativity, healing, increasing physical energy, hope, new beginnings, self-esteem, optimism, clear thinking, preventing nightmares

Clear Quartz: Amplification of psychic abilities and magick in general; may substitute for any stone in spellwork

Fluorite: Stability, order, discernment, concentration, clear thinking, reducing anger and depression, strengthening of all other stones

Garnet: Passion, courage, loyalty, devotion, love, stability, order

Geode: Astral travel

Hematite: Grounding, healing, balance, energy flow, stabilizing emotions, absorbing and grounding negative energy

Jade: Concentration, unconditional love, fidelity, harmony, health, justice, protection, luck, beauty, energy, stress relief, wisdom, growth, healthy perspective

Jasper: Protection, awareness, insight, grounding, love (red jasper), mental blockages (brown jasper), physical blockages (poppy jasper)

Jet: Protection, divination, goddess energy

Labradorite: Imagination, releasing inhibitions, self-confidence, communication with spirits, inner strength and courage, success, intuition illumination

Lace Agate: Joy, encouragement, optimism, self-acceptance, confidence, courage to speak the truth

Lapis Lazuli: Intelligence, communication, truth, deflecting negativity

Malachite: Transformation, clearing chakras, attracting love

Onyx: Self-control, confidence, mental strength, protection from negativity, grounding

Opalite: Self-worth, stabilizing mood swings, calming nerves

Pearl: A pure heart, peace, balance, emotions, lunar energy

Peridot: Astral work, protection from nightmares, emotional healing, inspiration, calm, banishing negative emotions, sleep

Petrified Wood: Grounding, strength, transformation

Pyrite: Intellect and memory, protection, shielding against negative energy

Rose Quartz: Love, happiness, friendship, fidelity, self-healing

Ruby: Love, nurturing, spirituality, protection, wealth, power

Sapphire: Beauty, insight, protection, prosperity, wisdom; hope and clarity of purpose (star sapphire)

Snowflake Obsidian: Protection, grounding, releasing negative energy such as anger, fear, jealousy, and greed

Sodalite: Communication, self-expression, self-esteem, awakening

Tiger's Eye: Courage, optimism, abundance, healing

Turquoise: Master healer, connecting to the Mind of the Universe, peace

Tea

Black Tea: Courage, strength

Chamomile: Love, healing, reducing stress

Cinnamon: Spirituality, success, healing, protection, power, love, luck, strength, prosperity

Coffee: Wealth, prosperity, love

Comfrey: Money, safety during travel, stability, endurance, matters relating to real estate or property

Ginger: Adventure and new experiences, sensuality, sexuality, personal confidence, prosperity, success

Ginseng: Love, beauty, protection, healing, lust

Green Tea: Healing, peace

Mugwort: Divination, astral travel, psychic power

Peppermint: Increasing the vibrations of a space; healing, purification

Yarn Texture

Bouclé: Lumps of soft at random intervals, bouclé represents surprise (the sixth element).

Chenille or Velvet: Pure luxury, chenille and velvet make you feel like a monarch: king, queen, or butterfly, your choice.

Cotton, 4-ply: This sturdy yarn doesn't stretch much. Worked in a tight stitch such as single crochet or stockinette, it would feel grounded and secure.

Fur: Fur offers warmth and comfort like your long-lost teddy bear.

Ribbon: Leaving interesting twists and turns, ribbon sparks the imagination.

Scrubby: Scrubby texture gives a small challenge to the senses to wake you up.

Wool Roving: Like fluffy clouds, this yarn adds whimsy.

Bibliography

Andrews, Ted. *How to Heal with Color*. St. Paul, MN: Llewellyn Publications, 2011.

Cunningham, Scott. *Cunningham's Encyclopedia of Crystal, Gem & Metal Magic*. St. Paul, MN: Llewellyn Publications, 1988.

———. *Cunningham's Encyclopedia of Magical Herbs*. St. Paul, MN: Llewellyn Publications, 1985.

Cunningham, Scott, and David Harrington. *Spell Crafts: Creating Magical Objects*. St. Paul, MN: Llewellyn, Publications, 1993.

Mountainwater, Shekhinah. *Ariadne's Thread: A Workbook of Goddess Magic*. Freedom, CA: The Crossing Press, 1996.

RavenWolf, Silver. *American Folk Magick, Charms, Spells, and Herbals*. St. Paul, MN: Llewellyn Publications, 1996.

———. *To Ride a Silver Broomstick*. St. Paul, MN: Llewellyn Publications, 1993.

Snow, Justine T. "The Spider's Web. Goddesses of Light and Loom: Examining the Evidence for the Indo-European Origin of Two Ancient Chinese Deities." *Sino-Platonic Papers* 118 (June 2002): 1–75. http://www.sino-platonic.org/complete/spp118_chinese_weaving_goddess.pdf.

Worwood, Valerie Ann. *The Complete Book of Essential Oils and Aromatherapy*. Novato, CA: New World Library, 1991.

Notes

Notes

Notes

Notes

Notes

Notes

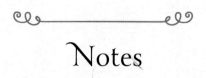

Notes